JESUS THE PHARISEE

A New Look at the Jewishness of Jesus

Harvey Falk

PAULIST PRESS
New York/Mahwah

Library of Congress
Catalog Card Number 84-61977

ISBN: 0-8091-2677-X

Published by Paulist Press
997 Macarthur Boulevard
Mahwah, N.J. 07430

Printed and bound in the United States of America

CONTENTS

DEDICATION

In Loving Memory
of My Grandparents

Eleazar and Chaya Falk
Menachem Mendl and Chana Eisen

Who Perished During the Holocaust

MAY THEIR SOULS
BE BOUND UP
IN THE BOND OF LIFE

Hillel said: Be Thou of the Disciples
of Aaron, One Who Loves Peace,
Pursues Peace, Loves Mankind, and
Brings Them Nigh to the Torah.

AVOT 1:12

TRACTATES OF MISHNAH AND TALMUD REFERRED TO IN THIS BOOK

Arakhin
Avodah Zarah
Avot
Avot D'Rabbi Nathan
Bava Batra
Bava Kamma
Bava Mezia
Bekhorot
Berakhot
Betsah
Demai
Eduyyot
Eruvin
Gittin
Hagigah
Hullin
Ketubbot
Kiddushin
Ma'asrot

Machshirin
Menahot
Mo'ed Katan
Nazir
Nedarim
Niddah
Parah
Pesahim
Rosh Ha-Shana
Sanhedrin
Shabbat
Shekalim
Sotah
Sukkah
Ta'anit
Terumot
Yadayim
Yevamot
Yoma

PREFACE

This book presents in a unique and scholarly way how the original founders of Christianity who were Jews were deeply involved in the customs and traditions of the Jewish heritage. Rabbi Falk traces the discussions between the various schools of learning, and especially the Schools of Hillel and Shammai. This scholarly approach shows how the founders of Christianity were well familiar with Jewish scholarship which affected much of Christian thought and teachings. Recent archaeological discoveries, especially the Dead Sea Scrolls, support the author's scholarly presentation.

The reader may ultimately ask why this approach by Rabbi Falk was not stressed in earlier times, for much hatred and persecution could have been avoided if students of this era understood the real facts of the historical development. It is most likely that the early rabbis were aware of this presentation, but feared their Christian neighbors' reaction. It is interesting that such great scholars as Moses Maimonides, Jacob Emden and others did back up in their great scholarly works this approach.

This book, which offers a new scholarly approach to Christian-Jewish relations, should be of great help to teachers and students in the field in order to get a better understanding of the importance of Judaism as it relates to early Christianity.

Prof. Abraham I. Katsh

INTRODUCTION

As the reader may note on an earlier page, this book is dedicated in memory of my grandparents who perished during the Holocaust. They were God-fearing, hard-working people, whose most cherished aim in life was to raise a happy and healthy family dedicated to the ancient traditions of their people. I know this, because I've heard much about them from my parents. My mother and father were fortunate enough to come to this blessed land as youngsters, and raise their children here. But my grandparents never made it to these shores. Neither did many other relatives of mine, who also perished in the forests, fields and concentration camps of war-torn Europe. Some died in Poland, some in other countries—countries with predominantly Christian populations.

Could the Holocaust have taken place on some other continent, in a non-Christian climate? Was it coincidental that the greatest crime in history perpetrated by man against his fellow man occurred in Christian countries? I cannot answer this question. But it is fairly common knowledge that the Christian Bible contains many passages that can be interpreted in an anti-Jewish manner. Jesus of Nazareth—upon whose life and teachings Christianity was founded—appears to have made certain strong statements against his fellow Jews, and especially against their rabbis. He denounced these rabbis' traditions, argued with them concerning Jewish laws, and was finally sentenced by a Jewish court who handed him over to the Romans for execution. All of this is recorded quite clearly in the Christian Gospels. I think it therefore safe to say

1

that if I were a Christian and understood the Gospels in such a manner, I would find it difficult to love my Jewish neighbors in my heart.

Many students of history have therefore concluded that the Holocaust was a natural climax to centuries of anti-Jewish feeling among Christians. The fuel for the fire of destruction had been accumulating for hundreds of years, until all that remained was for someone to light the match. Germany's problems and the leaders they produced ignited the flames. These historians might therefore argue that the Holocaust was not so much a German-Jewish affair, as it was a Christian-Jewish catastrophe.

Many books have been written on the Holocaust and Christian anti-Semitism. But the most positive element of this recent activity would seem to be that many of these works are being written or published by Christians. Christian scholars, writers and thinkers are devoting their time and efforts to achieve a better relationship with the Jewish community. And this in turn brings about a reciprocal approach among Jews, even among those who suffered during the Holocaust: memories of Christians who helped Jews escape their persecutors, even at the risk of their own lives; memories of Christians who gave shelter to Jewish children in their homes, representing them as their own. And many of these Christians have related that they felt closer to the founder of their faith, Jesus of Nazareth, when helping their Jewish friends and neighbors. It is similarly apparent from the writings of many contemporary Christian theologians that they are discovering new insights when concentrating on the Jewishness of Jesus.

Perhaps then we have entered into a new era in Christian-Jewish relations. Christians are in fact asking Jews to assist them in their search for the Jewish underpinnings of their faith. There is no question that Jews can contribute to this no-ble cause, for it is they who continue to study and practice the ancient traditions—traditions adhered to and studied by such important Christian figures as Jesus of Nazareth, Paul of Tarsus, Peter the first Pope, and others.

This is not to say that Jews are rushing en masse to answer the Christian call. It is a new phenomenon, and considering the dismal record of Jewish-Christian relations over the past two thousand years, some wariness is to be expected. In conversations with fellow Jews and rabbis, I have encountered reservations to dialogue. There is the argument that Christians are themselves in shock at the extent of the Holocaust's dimensions; but human nature has a way of coming to terms with shock, and a Jewish response might eventually even backfire. Some—especially those who spent their early years in Europe—simply can't believe that Christians are sincerely seeking better relations with Jews. Some have openly expressed a fear that dialogue is a subtle attempt at converting Jews.

Let me then begin by emphasizing that this work has not been written in haste. The research and writing leading up to it have occupied me for a period of years. I have also had the opportunity during that time to attend various meetings of Christians and Jews, and I am convinced that many Christians are extremely sincere in the movement toward dialogue. Perhaps my attitude toward Christians is also colored by my good fortune to have been born and raised in the United States and to have known many wonderful Christian people. I recall one Christian neighbor who was particularly kind to my family. All he would ask in return would be: "Remember me in your prayers." This Christian man has since passed away, but I often think of him.

On the scholarly level, Moses Maimonides (1135–1204)—one of the leading rabbinic figures in Jewish history—

was once asked whether Jews should engage in talks with
Christians concerning the Noahide Commandments—the
Commandments enjoined by the Torah upon the Gentiles—
which according to rabbinic tradition were given by God to
Adam and Noah. According to rabbinic teaching, those Gentiles who observe these precepts are assured their share in the
World to Come. It is thus important to note that rabbinic Judaism has always recognized two different religious codes:
the 613 precepts given to the Jews following their liberation
from Egypt, and the earlier Noahide system for all mankind.
(See the opening of Chapter 5 for further details concerning
the Noahide Commandments.) Maimonides encouraged
such dialogue with Christians. He reasoned that even if nothing positive develops from such talks, no harm will emerge
either, since "They will not find in their Torah (the Christian
Bible) anything that conflicts with our Torah."[1] When one
recognizes that very few rabbis would attempt to formulate a
Jewish point of view without first consulting Maimonides, the
relevance of his remark can be appreciated. (To be sure, Maimonides' works were burned by certain Jews when they first
appeared. Time is always required before new views can become recognized and accepted.)

But the work that inspired me most and truly laid the
groundwork for this book was a letter by the eighteenth century Talmudist Rabbi Jacob Emden, whose letter to the Polish
rabbinate of his time concerning early Christianity remains a
classic in the field. Emden wrote that Jesus never intended to
abolish Judaism, but only to establish a new religion for the
Gentiles based upon the ancient Noahide Commandments
transmitted by Moses at Mount Sinai. Emden asserted that Jesus brought about a double blessing to the world, by strengthening the Torah of Moses and at the same time removing
idolatry from the midst of the Gentiles. He also stressed that

Paul was a scholar, an attendant of Rabban Gamaliel the Elder. Rabbi Emden published the letter as an appendix to a larger work entitled *Seder Olam Rabbah Vezuta* (1757).

Unfortunately, Emden's thesis never gained a substantial following. The most obvious reason would seem to be the frequent harsh statements made by Jesus against the rabbis and Jews of his time. In a later book (*Sefer Shimmush,* 1758), Emden himself raised this question. The reply he offered was that Jesus and Paul recognized that the Gentiles were anti-Jewish by nature, and they wished to utilize these deeply ingrained feelings of the Gentiles in order to help propagate their new faith. However, Emden stressed that the founders of Christianity surely hoped that the spiritual teachings of their faith would ultimately cause Christians to support and cherish the Jews. Emden lamented that Christians have not come to understand this.[2] Emden's defense of his thesis does not seem to have gained acceptance in the scholarly community.

I first read Emden's letter in a library some years before the completion of this book. The document has never been reprinted in its original form and source, and I recall how careful I had to be while reading it so as not to crumple the two-century-old pages. The paper was deeply yellowed, and many letters had been obliterated. That document forged a lasting impression upon my imagination. I suppose that was mainly because it had been written by a renowned Talmudist and mystic, one whose books are still read avidly by many Jews in our own time. I have in fact translated Rabbi Emden's letter from the original Hebrew, along with a brief description of the events surrounding its composition. The letter and commentary have appeared in *The Journal of Ecumenical Studies,* and are included at the end of this chapter as an appendix.

As I sat in the brightly-lit library room savoring Emden's

words,[3] the first stirrings of my imagination began to take hold. My thoughts shifted to the Dead Sea Scrolls, those mysterious parchments found some two decades earlier which were still perplexing scholars. Many authorities have expressed a belief that Jesus and Paul were acquainted with the Essene authors—it is generally accepted that the Scrolls are of Essene origin—since many passages in the New Testament bear striking similarity to the Scrolls. But what especially baffled scholars was that the Essenes appear to have been extremely pious Jews, whereas Jesus and Paul had forsaken their Jewish origins. But what if Emden was right! I reasoned. The Talmud does record that Moses obligated the Jews to spread knowledge of the Noahide commandments to all mankind. What if the pious Essenes had attempted such a mission to the Gentiles, and Jesus and Paul had been successful in bringing their efforts to fruition? (Such an approach does not diminish in any manner from the centrality of the Gospels and Christian tradition for Christians. To the contrary, it obligates Christians all the more to search for the true meaning of Jesus' teachings—just as Jews must constantly search for the correct interpretation of their tradition.)

It was not until some time later that I discovered a passage in the Jerusalem Talmud recording that Menahem the Essene and one hundred and sixty disciples had left the Jewish community about 20 B.C.E. on a mission to the Gentiles. As a detective who finally sees his hunch materializing, I delved further. This Menahem had served as a vice-president of the Sanhedrin under the sage Hillel some thirty years before Jesus' birth. The Mishnah makes quite clear that Menahem subjected himself totally to Hillel's authority, thus establishing a first tenuous link between the Essenes and Hillel. Further links were to present themselves—such as the fact that the Essenes, as well as Hillel and members of his School, were known as Hasidim (not to be confused with the contemporary movement of Hasidim founded by Rabbi Israel Baal Shem Tov in the eighteenth-century). The Talmud in fact makes mention of a cave of the Hasidim and a scroll of the Hasidim—obvious references to the Essenes. Interestingly, Menahem the Essene left Hillel's Sanhedrin when the sage Shammai succeeded him, probably about 20 B.C.E.

Was Menahem forced out by Shammai and his followers? Were Menahem and his disciples the authors of the mysterious Damascus Document found among the Dead Sea Scrolls? Did Hillel's disciples join Menahem in his mission to the Gentiles? Did the later rabbis of the Talmud approve of Menahem's mission to the Gentiles? Was Shammai the "Teacher of Lies" criticized in the Damascus Document? These questions and many others will be addressed in this book. But one fact we know for certain. The first disputes regarding the Oral Law passed down for some seventeen hundred years from Moses at Sinai took place at this time between the sages Hillel and Shammai. Their respective Schools—Bet Hillel and Bet Shammai—were to clash over three hundred and fifty times on issues of the Oral Law during the next hundred years. Nor were these minor disputes; the issues between Bet Hillel and Bet Shammai went to the very core of what Judaism stood for—and especially important for our subject, Judaism's attitude toward the salvation of the Gentiles.

The Schools of Shammai and Hillel both accepted all of the commandments contained in the five books of the Torah. But the written law of Moses is too brief to be applied to practical issues of everyday life, and it was accepted that an oral and more detailed tradition was handed down by Moses. The debates of Bet Hillel and Bet Shammai centered on this oral tradition.

The School of Shammai burst upon the Jewish scene

some two decades before Jesus' birth, and flourished for approximately a hundred years. After the destruction of the Temple in Jerusalem in 70 C.E., the seat of the Sanhedrin was relocated to Yavneh, where Bet Hillel became established as the majority. Also at this time, a Heavenly Voice was heard declaring the Law to be decided in favor of Bet Hillel. Since that time all Jewry has accepted the teachings of Bet Hillel.

It shall be the goal of this book to demonstrate that Jesus' debates with the Pharisees were actually disputes recorded in the Talmud between Bet Shammai and Bet Hillel, with Jesus adopting the views of Bet Hillel. We shall also endeavor to prove that Bet Shammai were in control of Jewish life and institutions during most of the first century, and that the murderous Zealots, often represented in the priesthood in Jerusalem, were followers of Bet Shammai. We shall also attempt to demonstrate that the Shammaites were responsible for handing Jesus over to the Romans for the crucifixion, and that their decision was in violation of Jewish law.

What emerges from this study is a new scenario of the times of Jesus, Paul and the Apostles. The Romans had conquered the land of Israel during the century before Jesus' birth. The Jewish People knew from an ancient prophecy that their Temple in Jerusalem would be destroyed by the Gentile enemy. Bet Hillel believed that reaching out to the Gentiles was the correct approach. They maintained that righteous Gentiles merit salvation just as Jews do, and it was their hope that a mission to the gentiles could avert the destruction of their land. Bet Shammai however looked down upon the Gentile world, holding that not even the most righteous Gentile could merit a share in the World to Come. The Jewish People and their teachers have since declared Bet Shammai's views to be null and void, as did a Heavenly Voice toward the close of the first century. Bet Shammai were indeed the Pharisees and priests that Jesus of Nazareth and Paul of Tarsus had to contend with. We shall in fact seek to demonstrate that Paul the Apostle's insistence that Gentiles be admitted into the early Christian Church was based on Bet Hillel's position that righteous Gentiles merit salvation. (Paul had studied under Rabban Gamaliel the Elder, a grandson of Hillel.)

I should once again point out to Christian readers that this book does not seek to change any basic Christian belief or dogma. To the contrary, Rabbi Emden's thesis demands that Christians search for the true traditions and teachings bequeathed to them by Jesus and his Apostles. This book only seeks to demonstrate that the apparently anti-Jewish passages contained in the New Testament were directed against the Shammaites, and not the Judaism of today which follows Bet Hillel.

Since much of this book deals with rabbinic sources, a brief history of this literature is in order—especially for Christian readers. Traditional Judaism holds that an oral tradition was passed down by Moses, which was forbidden to be set to writing. It was this Oral Law that later caused controversy among the rabbis—and especially between Bet Shammai and Bet Hillel. Finally, out of fear it would be forgotten, the sages permitted it to be committed to writing. The first major works were the Mishnah (second century C.E.) and the Tosefta (fourth century), followed by the two Talmuds—the Babylonian Talmud and the Jerusalem Talmud (fifth century)—with the Babylonian version for various reasons gaining somewhat more popularity than the Jerusalem. Hence, all references to Talmud in this work are to the Babylonian, unless specified as Jerusalem. Also at this time, books of homilies known as Midrash began to appear. The two major commentaries to the Babylonian Talmud are those of Rashi (Rabbi Solomon Ben Isaac, French rabbi, 1040–1105) and the Tosafists (European rabbinic works, principally during the two centuries following Rashi)—without which the Talmud would have remained virtually inaccessible. As for the codification of the Talmudic discussions and debates into final legal form, Moses Maimonides (1135–1204) is recognized as the most comprehensive authority, while Rabbi Joseph Caro's (1488–1575) *Shulhan Arukh* has also gained universal acceptance. This book will refer to the works of many other rabbinic scholars, and a brief biography of each appears at the end of the book. It should be mentioned here that the Mishnah and the Babylonian Talmud have been translated into the English language.

It is important for the reader to recognize that the Mishnah, Talmud and Tosefta are the works of primary interest and authority when researching Jewish law and tradition. At the same time, we must realize that it is virtually impossible to understand these works properly without consulting later rabbinic sources.

This book was written over a period of years, and is the result of much research. The reader may find some repetition, and may even wonder why some passages in later chapters weren't incorporated into the book earlier. However, I have tried to form the book along the order in which the thoughts came to me, thus enabling the reader to share some of the excitement of discovery.

As the writing progressed, I sought to discuss my ideas with prominent scholars. I would like to thank the following for giving me of their time and counsel: Professor Abraham I. Katsh; Dr. Sid Leiman, professor of Jewish History and Literature at Brooklyn College; Dr. Sidney Schulman, noted Talmudic scholar and author; Dr. Michael Wyschogrod, professor and chairman of the Department of Philosophy, Baruch College, City University of New York.

I should also take this opportunity to express my appreciation to my editor, Father Lawrence Boadt, C.S.P., for his valuable suggestions.

But above all I owe a debt of gratitude to my wife and children who graciously gave me of the time and attention which was rightfully theirs.

Harvey Falk
New York City
1984

NOTES

1. Responsa of Maimonides, No. 364, pp. 331–332, Freimann Edition, 1934.

    However, Maimonides dissuaded such discussion with Moslems because of their views regarding the Torah, fearing that harm might result to Jewish residents in Moslem lands (*ibid.*). Despite this, he spoke highly of Moslems as being halakhic counterparts of the biblical *Ger Toshav* (a Gentile who formally accepted the seven Noahide Commandments); see Maimonides, *Yad, Ma'akhalot Asurot* 11:7. Cf. chapter Hillel's Convert Revisited for a more detailed study of the Ger Toshav institution.

2. *Sefer Shimmush* has been republished by Hebrew University (1974), and Emden included in it additional commentary to his original letter (pp. 29–41). His explanation for the anti-Jewish statements contained in the Gospels appears on page 33.

3. Samson Raphael Hirsch, the illustrious German Jewish leader, quotes further from R. Emden's writings in the tractate Avot: "Christians and Moslems must be regarded as an instrument for the fulfillment of the prophecy that the knowledge of God will one day spread throughout the earth. . . . And Christian scholars have not only won acceptance among the nations for the written

Revelation but have also helped to protect God's orally transmitted Revelation. For when in their hostility to the Law ruthless persons in our own midst sought to abrogate and uproot the Talmud, others from their midst rose to defend it and to repulse these attempts" (*Judaism Eternal*, Volume 2, pp. 169–170).

1.

RABBI JACOB EMDEN'S
VIEWS ON CHRISTIANITY*

Rabbi Jacob Emden (1697–1776) was one of the leading Torah authorities of the past several centuries. Historians of the
rabbinate have often compared him to Maimonides, both
having written on all branches of Jewish knowledge, and both
having shared a pragmatic and even innovative approach.
Even those who disagreed with him sought his opinion, and
he is read with interest to this day. Thus, Moses Mendelssohn,
founder of the *Haskalah* (Enlightenment) movement, wrote to
him as "your disciple, who thirsts for your words." Although
Emden did not approve of the Hasidic movement—which
had its beginnings in his time—his books are highly regarded
amongst Hasidim. R. M. Sofer referred to him as a "prophet"
(*Hatam Sofer* 6:59). Thirty-one works were published during
his lifetime, ten posthumously, while others remain in manuscript. In his time, he was a fearless champion of Orthodox
Judaism.

His scholarly stature and endless quest for truth were
surely the catalysts responsible for catapulting him into the fore-
front of the battle against the Shabbatean messianic movement. (Shabbetai Zevi, a seventeenth-century mystic [d.
1676], represented himself as the Messiah, and many Jews initially believed his claim. When the Turks threatened him
with death unless he converted to Islam, he meekly ac-

*Reprinted from the *Journal of Ecumenical Studies*, 19:1, Winter 1982

quiesced, expiring in ignominy. However, secret cells of believers still followed his teachings and hoped for new
leadership.) Emden charged R. Jonathan Eybeschuetz, another leading German rabbi of his time, with being a secret
follower of the heretical sect, causing an upheaval among European Jewry. Rabbis and community leaders joined the fray,
and Emden was once forced to flee for his life. The accusation, followed by excommunications, caused what was probably the greatest rabbinic *cause célèbre* of modern times.

Also in R. Emden's time, a group of Polish Shabbateans
under the leadership of Jacob Frank posed an enormous
threat to the Jewish community of Poland. This group—dis-
torting various Kabbalistic formulas—violated Jewish law and
practiced sexual immorality. When excommunicated by the
Polish rabbinate, they complained to several Catholic bishops
that they were being persecuted by their fellow Jews because
they believed in the Trinity. This eventually led to the burning of the Talmud in Poland. The Frankists also sought to revive the notorious blood libel against the Jews.

During this last controversy, the Council of the Four
Lands—the central institution of Jewish self-government in
Poland—turned to Rabbi Emden for guidance. The basic
question was whether it was permitted to inform the Polish
authorities—both governmental and ecclesiastical—about the
true nature of the Frankists. Rabbi Emden not only replied
that it was their obligation to do so, no matter what the con-
sequences, but he also advised them to appeal to the Christian
community for help in the struggle against the immoral
Frankists and generally to aid the Jews in their observance of
the Torah. This led Emden into a thorough analysis of the beginnings of Christianity and especially the original intentions
of Jesus and Paul. He believed that Jesus and the Apostle to
the Gentiles acted entirely within the Halakha (Jewish law) in
creating a religion for the Gentiles based on the Noahide

Commandments, and he interpreted various passages in the Gospels to show that both considered Jewish law eternally binding upon Jews. (The basic seven Noahide Commandments consist of the prohibitions against idolatry, blasphemy, killing, stealing, sexual sins, eating the limb of a living animal [cruelty to animals], and the imperative to establish courts of justice. According to the Talmud and Tosefta, those Gentiles who observe these statutes are considered to be of the Hasidim [pious ones] of the Nations and to merit a share in the World to Come.) Although many Jewish authorities have written positively concerning Christianity, it is clear that Emden went much further. He wrote that Jesus "brought about a double kindness to the world" and that "Paul was a scholar, an attendant of Rabban Gamaliel the Elder."

It might be argued that R. Emden wrote this letter at a time of great turmoil and that he may have abandoned his position at a later date. It would be erroneous to assume so, as he frequently reiterated his positive views concerning Christianity—and Islam as well—in his other books. Commenting on the passage, "May all inhabitants of the earth recognize and know . . .," in the *Alenu* prayer, Emden wrote: "The proper reason for these words is to pray for the Gentiles; we witness here the greatness of our Sages and their magnanimity toward all mankind, to long for their welfare, and to plead mercifully for their true success" (Siddur). Taking note of the Mishnah in Avot 4:11, "Every assembly that is for the sake of Heaven will in the end be established," he wrote: "Their assembly (Christianity and Islam) is also for the sake of Heaven, to make Godliness known amongst the nations, to speak of Him in distant places; they have accepted virtually all of the Noahide Commandments, aside from many fine practices which they have endorsed and accepted; He grants prophecy to those who have sanctified themselves sufficiently" (*Lechem Shamayim*).

His letter to the Polish Council appeared as an appendix to his *Seder Olam* (1757) and was republished in his *Sefer Shimmush*. In his autobiography (*Megillat Sefer*, pp. 185–186), Emden noted that his arch-rival, R. J. Eybeschuetz, accused him of heresy because of his positive views on Christianity and that certain of his followers succeeded to some extent in discouraging sales of the book. This did not faze Emden in the least, and, after excoriating Eybeschuetz, he concluded (ibid., p. 189): "Upon us will God cause His sun to rise, and upon us shall be seen the Light and Holy One of Israel."

In order properly to evaluate the importance of this document, one has to first consider the reticence of most Orthodox Jews to enter into a dialogue with Christians. While this may be ascribed to various reasons, not least among them is the paucity of writing concerning Christianity by recognized Jewish authorities—the term "recognized" implying such as are universally acknowledged as Torah sages by all Jewry, even the ultra-orthodox. Traditional Jews historically have not taken positions on major issues, especially one of the magnitude of dialogue, without examining the opinions of these savants. Rabbi Emden was such a figure.

As all leaders in history who became enmeshed in controversies, Rabbi Jacob Emden has not escaped criticism. Some liberal rabbis have evidently seen in him a prototype of the unyielding Orthodox rabbi, because he refused to compromise in any manner with those movements he considered threatening to traditional Judaism. Even some Orthodox rabbis have never forgiven him his attacks on R. Jonathan Eybeschuetz. But, to most of Jewry for over two hundred years now, he remains affectionately known as R. Jacob, and many Jewish homes count his books—especially his prayer book—among their prized possessions.

The early and final sections of the letter, which deal with the Shabbateans and the internal situation in Poland, are omitted from the translation. The passages on Christianity are given in full.

RABBI JACOB EMDEN'S LETTER
(SEDER OLAM RABBAH VEZUTA)

For it is recognized that also the Nazarene and his disciples, especially Paul, warned concerning the Torah of the Israelites, to which all the circumcised are tied. And if they are truly Christians, they will observe their faith with truth, and not allow within their boundary this new unfit Messiah Shabbetai Zevi who came to destroy the earth.

But truly even according to the writers of the Gospels, a Jew is not permitted to leave his Torah, for Paul wrote in his letter to the Galatians (Gal. 5) "I, Paul, say to you that if you receive circumcision, the Messiah will do you no good at all. You can take it from me that every man who receives circumcision is under obligation to keep the entire Torah." Again because of this he admonished in a letter to the Corinthians (1 Cor. 7) that the circumcised should not remove the marks of circumcision, nor should the uncircumcised circumcise themselves.

Many have asked that Paul appears to contradict himself here. In the Acts of the Apostles (Acts 16), it is mentioned that Paul circumcised his disciple Timothy. And they found this very puzzling, for this act seems to contradict the later text which seems to indicate that he considered circumcision a temporary commandment until the Messiah's arrival; but this took place after the time of the Nazarene! Therefore you must realize—and accept the truth from him who speaks it—that we see clearly here that the Nazarene and his Apostles did not wish to destroy the Torah from Israel, God forbid; for it is written so in Matthew (Mt. 5), the Nazarene having said,

"Do not suppose that I have come to abolish the Torah. I did not come to abolish, but to fulfill. I tell you this: So long as heaven and earth endure, not a letter, not a stroke, will disappear from the Torah until it is achieved. If any man therefore sets aside even the least of the Torah's demands, and teaches others to do the same, he will have the lowest place in the Kingdom of Heaven, whereas anyone who keeps the Torah, and teaches others so, will stand high in the Kingdom of Heaven." This is also recorded in Luke (Lk. 16). It is therefore exceedingly clear that the Nazarene never dreamed of destroying the Torah.

We similarly find Paul, his disciple, in a letter to the Corinthians (1 Cor. 5), accusing them of fornication, and condemning one who had lived with his father's wife. You may therefore understand that Paul doesn't contradict himself because of his circumcision of Timothy, for the latter was the son of a Jewish mother and a Gentile father (Acts 16), and Paul was a scholar, an attendant of Rabban Gamaliel the Elder, well-versed in the laws of the Torah. He knew that the child of a Jewish mother is considered a full Jew, even if the father should be a Gentile, as is written in the Talmud and Codes. He therefore acted entirely in accordance with the Halakha by circumcising Timothy. This would be in line with his position that all should remain within their own faith (1 Cor. 7). Timothy, born of a Jewish mother, had the law of a Jew, and had to be circumcised, just as he was enjoined to observe all commandments of the Torah (Paul's condemnation of the man who lived with his stepmother is similarly understandable, as such an act is also forbidden to Noahides), for all who are circumcised are bound by all the commandments. This provides a satisfactory reply to the question.

This will also solve the apparent contradictions in the Nazarene's own statements. Christian scholars have assumed from certain passages in the Gospels that he wished to give a new Torah to take the place of the Torah of Moses. How could he then have said explicitly that he comes only to fulfill it? But it is as I have said earlier—that the writers of the Gospels never meant to say that the Nazarene came to abolish Judaism, but only that he came to establish a religion for the Gentiles from that time onward. Nor was it new, but actually ancient; they being the Seven Commandments of the Sons of Noah, which were forgotten. The Apostles of the Nazarene then established them anew. However, those born as Jews, or circumcised as converts to Judaism (Ex. 12:49; one law shall be to him that is home-born, and unto the stranger) are obligated to observe all commandments of the Torah without exception.

But for the Gentiles he reserved the Seven Commandments which they have always been obligated to fulfill. It is for that reason that they were forbidden pollutions of idols, fornication, blood, and things strangled (Acts 15). They also forbade them circumcision and the Sabbath. All of this was in accord with the law and custom of our Torah, as expounded by our Sages, the true transmitters from Moses at Sinai. It was they who sat upon his seat (as the Nazarene himself attested [Mt. 23]). It was they (the Sages or Pharisees) who said that it is forbidden to circumcise a Gentile who does not accept upon himself the yoke of (all) the commandments. The Sages likewise said that the Gentile is enjoined not (fully) to observe the Sabbath. The Apostles of the Nazarene therefore chose for those Gentiles who do not enter the Jewish faith that instead of circumcision they should practice immersion (for truly immersion is also a condition of full conversion), and a commemoration of the Sabbath was made for them on Sunday.

But the Nazarene and his Apostles observed the Sabbath and circumcision as mentioned earlier, for they were born as Jews. They observed the Torah fully, until after a period of time a few of them decided to give up the Torah among themselves completely. They said that its observance was too difficult for them and agreed to remove its yoke from their necks (Acts 15).

But even here they did correctly as far as the Gentiles were concerned, for they were not commanded to observe it. Nor is it proper to make it difficult for them, since they did not receive (accept?) the Torah and are not enjoined to observe the 613 commandments. However, it is completely different as far as the Jews are concerned, for they became obligated to fulfill the Torah because God delivered them from the iron furnace (Egypt) to be the people of his possession. Therefore they and their children became subject to it forever. This, their covenant, will not be forgotten from their mouths, nor be discontinued from their children. For it they have given their lives throughout the generations, as the Psalmist has recorded (Ps. 44:18): All this is come upon us; yet have we not forgotten Thee, neither have we been false to Thy covenant.

Certainly, therefore, there is no doubt that one who seeks truth will agree with our thesis, that the Nazarene and his Apostles never meant to abolish the Torah of Moses from one who was born a Jew. Likewise did Paul write in his letter to the Corinthians (1 Cor. 7) that each should adhere to the faith in which each was called. They therefore acted in accordance with the Torah by forbidding circumcision to Gentiles, according to the Halakha, as it is forbidden to one who does not accept the yoke of the commandments. They knew that it would be too difficult for the Gentiles to observe the Torah of Moses. They therefore forbade them to circumcise, and it would suffice that they observe the Seven Noahide Commandments, as commanded upon them through the Halakha from Moses at Sinai.

It is therefore a habitual saying of mine (not as a hypocritical flatterer, God forbid, for I am of the faithful believers of Israel, and I know well that the remnant of Israel will not speak falsehood, nor will their mouths contain a deceitful tongue) that the Nazarene brought about a double kindness in the world. On the one hand, he strengthened the Torah of Moses majestically, as mentioned earlier, and not one of our Sages spoke out more emphatically concerning the immutability of the Torah. And on the other hand, he did much good for the Gentiles (provided they do not turn about his intent as they please, as some foolish ones have done because they did not fully understand the intent of the authors of the Gospels. I have recently seen someone publish a book, and he had no idea about what he was writing. For if he had understood the subject, he would have kept his silence and not wasted the paper and ink. There are also found among us foolish scholars who know not their right from their left in the Written and Oral Torahs and cause the people to err with their pompous pronouncements. But there are true scholars among the Christians, just as there are the chosen few among Torah scholars; and there are few of the truly great.) by doing away with idolatry and removing the images from their midst. He obligated them with the Seven Commandments so that they should not be as the beasts of the field. He also bestowed upon them ethical ways, and in this respect he was much more stringent with them than the Torah of Moses, as is well-known. This in itself was most proper, as it is the correct way to acquire ethical practices, as the philosopher (Maimonides) mentioned. We have written similarly in our Siddur. However, it is not necessary to impose upon Jews such extreme ethical practices, since they have been obligated to the yoke of Torah, which weakens the strength of the (evil) inclination without it. They have taken the oath at Sinai and are already trained in proper practice and nature. These are clear words that will not be rejected by a clear-thinking person.

If certain Christians who consider themselves scholars

would understand this secret, who believe that they are commanded to abolish the Torah of Moses from the seed of Israel, they would not engage in such foolishness. The people listen to their self-conceived words, something which was never intended by the writers of the Gospels. Quite the opposite, they have written clearly that they intended the contrary.

Because of these errant scholars, hatred has increased toward the Jews who are blameless of any guilt and proceed innocently to observe their Torah with all their heart, imbued with the fear of God. They should instead bring their people to love the ancient Children of Israel who remain loyal to their God, as indeed commanded to Christians by their original teachers.

They even said to love one's enemies. How much more so to us! In the name of heaven, we are your brothers! One God has created us all. Why should they abuse us because we are joined to the commandments of God, to which we are tied with the ropes of his love? We do this not to enjoy the pleasures of the (evil) inclination and emptiness of a passing world. For truly (Ps. 44) we have become a byword among the nations, and with all this (ibid.). In God have we gloried all the day, and we will give thanks unto Thy name for ever. We pray for the good of the entire world, and especially for the benefit of these lands in which we reside, protecting us and our observance of the Torah . . .

You, members of the Christian faith, how good and pleasant it might be if you will observe that which was commanded to you by your first teachers; how wonderful is your share if you will assist the Jews in the observance of their Torah. You will truly receive reward as if you had fulfilled it yourselves—for the one who helps others to observe is greater than one who observes but does not help others to do so—

even though you only observe the Seven Commandments. I have written similarly in my pleasant work *Torat Ha-Kena'ot*—that the Jew who observes the Torah, but doesn't support it, is considered among the cursed; and the Gentile who does not observe the 613 commandments, but supports it, is considered among the blessed.

Translated by Harvey Falk

2

HILLEL'S CONVERT REVISITED—
A SECOND LOOK

Many Jews are familiar since childhood with the Talmud's almost anecdotal treatment (Shabbat 31A) of the three heathens who appeared before the two leading rabbis of their time, Hillel and Shammai, for the purpose of conversion. To recapitulate, the first was interested in accepting only the written law's authority, but not the oral tradition; the second, and most famous, asked to be taught the entire Torah while standing on one foot, while the third aspired to become a convert so that he might attain the office of high priest. We recall almost with nostalgia how Shammai rebuffed them harshly, while Hillel's gentleness and patient instruction won them over to Judaism. Hillel and Shammai flourished during the era of the Second Temple, or end of first century B.C.E. and beginning of first century C.E.

A closer examination of the Talmudic text raises difficult questions. The second heathen surely ranks as one of the greatest pranksters of all time; to be taught the entire Torah while standing on one foot indeed! Since a rabbi's appraisal of the potential convert's sincerity is of paramount importance[1] in his decision on whether to proceed with the rite, one finds Hillel's interest in him rather surprising. Many rabbis would have surely shown him the door, as Shammai did.

Shammai's actions as well are rather baffling. He scolded the first heathen and had him removed from the premises,

24

whereas the latter two were repulsed with a builder's measuring rod. Scholars have adduced from this passage that the sage was either in the building business or a carpenter by trade. Now does it sound logical for a rabbi who surely had to reply to religious queries from Jews throughout the world, and who led one of the two leading yeshivot (Bet Shammai), to have also been engaged in the building trade? And where was that measuring rod when the first heathen appeared? Why didn't he use it on him as well? Too, one of Shammai's favorite teachings was (Avot 1:15) to receive all men with a cheerful countenance. Was it generally his practice to use his building rod on those he disagreed with?

And Hillel's instruction to the famed second heathen defies comprehension. To his request to be taught the entire Torah while standing on one foot, Hillel replied, "What is hateful unto thee, do not unto thy neighbor—this is the entire Torah; the rest is commentary."

This jolting negative metaphoric contraction of the 613 commandments of the Torah finds no counterpart in Talmudic literature. Rashi offers two interpretations: that God is referred to in scripture as "neighbor"[2] or "friend," or that the prohibitions of theft, adultery and "most commandments" of the Torah can be classified in this vein. The mere fact that Rashi offers two interpretations is usually a signal of a difficult text.

Later commentators adopted the more literal view that Hillel was referring to the Golden Rule, love thy neighbor as thyself (Leviticus 19:18), but his reference to it in a negative form was in order to incorporate certain halakhic principles into the teaching.[3]

Contemporary rabbis are all too familiar with the problems of conversions, and it would seem that any rabbi found nowadays giving such instructions to a potential convert would surely draw suspicion, if not wrath, from traditionalists. Hillel, despite his habitual more lenient attitude in halakhic matters, was one of the guardians of the oral tradition in his time, and his renowned statement to the "one-footed" convert has challenged and puzzled scholars for centuries.

In order to solve these questions, I should like to offer a fundamentally different interpretation to the text, most specifically to the position of the second convert. A prefatory note to the subject of conversions would first be in order. Two types of converts existed in ancient times, the *Ger Tzedek* and the *Ger Toshav*, whereas only the first is accepted nowadays. The *Ger Tzedek* accepts all 613 commandments of the Torah, and after circumcision and/or ritual immersion is recognized as a full Jew. The *Ger Toshav* of ancient times obligated himself only to the seven Noahide Commandments, after which he was permitted to settle in the Land of Israel, and the Jewish community became liable to see to his economic well-being.[4]

Judaism considers the seven Noahide Commandments to be the cornerstones of all religion and civilization, having been incumbent upon the human race since the time of Adam. Rabbi Joshua of Hillel's School gave their opinion—and all Jewry nowadays accepts the opinion of Bet Hillel—that a non-Jew who accepts these Commandments as divinely ordained and practices them is considered one of the Hasidim (righteous ones) of the Nations, and merits a share in the World to Come.[5] Judaism has always viewed other religions from the perspective of whether or not they conform to the Noahide commandments.

According to scripture (Exodus 23:33), idolators were not permitted to live in ancient Israel, lest they cause the people to sin. If a Gentile wished to settle there, he would appear before three learned men, accept the Noahide Laws, and would then be permitted to settle[6] with the status of a *Ger Toshav*. It is my opinion that Hillel's famed convert sought this status. When he inquired to be taught the entire Torah while standing on one foot, he was not jesting; he was referring to the seven Noahide Commandments, which can indeed be imparted in a brief span of time. (The commentaries have always taken for granted that each of the three wished to become a *Ger Tzedek*.)

Hillel's reply is to be similarly understood. By "thy neighbor," the sage was referring to the second parties involved—God, one's fellow man, and the animal world as well. He was actually offering a brief synopsis of the Noahide Commandments.[7]

Having ascertained Hillel's position, we shall now turn to Shammai and his use of the "measuring rod" on this heathen.

Rabbi Eliezer ben Hyrcanus, a leading sage of the first century C.E., was a member of the School of Shammai.[8] Following a well-known debate with the sages,[9] he was excommunicated for refusing to accept the authority of the majority opinion. To his last day, he insisted that he had never stated aught that he had not received from his teachers,[10] and would bend to no man. Among these minority views was his opinion[11] that a Gentile who observes the Noahide commandments does not merit a share in the World to Come. We may therefore assume with surety that this was also the stance of the School of Shammai and Shammai himself, especially considering Shammai's stance toward the converts here.[12]

Students of Talmud are well acquainted with the narrator's use of satiric metaphors (*Melitza*). When the heathen requested the sage to instruct him concerning the Noahide Commandments, Shammai would have advised him that a *Ger Toshav*, or observant Noahide, receives no reward in the afterlife. It was this figurative "measuring rod" (i.e., observe, but no immortality) that repulsed the Gentile. The allusion to the tool is not, however, to be taken literally.[13]

Too, Shammai used the same "measuring rod" on the third heathen, by advising him that a *Ger Tzedek* had no rights to the high priesthood. Hillel gently pointed out that any Jew not born as a *Kohen* (descendant of Aaron) was similarly not entitled to the office. This calmed the heathen, and he converted.

In the case of the first convert, who expressed an interest in the written law but not the oral tradition, a blatant example of heresy, Shammai simply threw him out. No "measuring rod" is involved here. Hillel's gentleness won him over as well.

The gratitude of the two *Ger Tzedeks* and the "one-footed" *Ger Toshav* to Hillel are well expressed in the Talmud's concluding comment: Some time later the three met in one place; said they, Shammai's impatience sought to drive us from the world, but Hillel's gentleness brought us under the wings of the *Shekhinah* (Divine Presence).

Our new interpretation of Hillel's heathen requires one further obstacle to be cleared: Did the institution of the *Ger Toshav* still exist during the period of the Second Temple, when Hillel flourished? Two corollary Talmudic statements might initially seem to challenge the assumption. The first (Arakhin 32b) posits that the laws of the Jubilee Year (freeing of slaves and reverting of sold land to its original owners) do not apply unless all the inhabitants of the Land of Israel dwell there. The second states (Arakhin 29a) that the acceptance of the *Ger Toshav* is only practiced when the Jubilee Year is in force. Since the two tribes of Reuben and Gad as well as half the tribe of Manasseh were exiled 151 years before the destruction of the First Temple, it would appear at first glance that the *Ger Toshav* was not accepted during the Second Temple period.

However, a study of the halakhic authorities suggests three possible motives for the heathen's appearance before Hillel:

1. According to R. Jacob Tam (Tosafists, Gittin 36a), the rules of the Jubilee Year were in full force during the Second Temple period. The Talmud's requirement that "all its inhabitants" be dwelling in the land was satisfied, as members of all twelve tribes were present in the country at the time.[14] Since the Jubilee Year was in force, so was the institution of the *Ger Toshav*.

2. According to Maimonides (*Shmittin* 10:8), the Jubilee Year was discontinued following the exile of the two and a half tribes, since the nation no longer dwelled within the original boundaries allotted to the twelve tribes by Joshua. However, R. Abraham Ben David of Posquieres (Rabad) rules (*Avodat Kochavim* 10:6) that although the community was no longer obligated to see to the financial well-being of the *Ger Toshav*, acceptance of the seven Commandments still entitled him to settle in the land—the rationale being that scripture's concern over the idolator's leading others to sin is satisfied. According to R. Joseph Caro—author of the *Shulhan Arukh*—in his commentary *Kesef Mishnah* to Maimonides (*ibid.*), the latter agreed with Rabad. Rashi (Arakhin 29a) appears to accept this view as well.[15]

Hence, the heathen appeared before Hillel to accept the Noahide Commandments and receive permission to settle in *Eretz Israel.*[16]

3. R. Joseph Babad (*Minhat Hinnukh*, no. 94) disagrees with *Kesef Mishnah*'s interpretation of Maimonides, and believes that the latter would not permit settlement of an observant Noahide after discontinuance of the Jubilee.[17]

According to *Minhat Hinnukh,* we would have to say that the heathen appeared before Hillel in order to learn the seven Commandments, so that he might be accounted among the Hasidim of the Nations, and merit a share in the World to Come. The Talmud's use of the term conversion (*Gerut*) with regard to the heathen would not be in the formal sense, but is rather understood as the transformation of a pagan into an observant Noahide.

A MISSION TO THE GENTILES BY THE HASIDIM

Although Judaism never attempted to missionize for converts to its religion, the discussion of the Talmud (Sanhedrin 57a) and especially Maimonides (*Melakhim,* Chap. 8) would seem to indicate that Moses obligated the Jews to spread knowledge of the Noahide commandments to all mankind. It is surprising, then, that no historical record exists recording such an endeavor. Especially in ancient times, when the world was mired in pagan and barbaric beliefs, one would have expected such a movement.

I have previously presented Rabbi Jacob Emden's view (*Sefer Shimmush* and Appendix to *Seder Olam*) that the original intent of Jesus and Paul was to bring the seven Noahide Commandments to the Gentiles, while the Jews should continue their adherence to Judaism. His view is generally unknown outside scholarly circles, although it is recorded in the three major Jewish encyclopedias (*Universal Jewish Encyclopedia* 3:190, *Jewish Encyclopedia* 5:623, and *Judaica* 3:198).

It might be mentioned here that most scholars have rejected R. Emden's stance. Nor is it my intention here to discuss the pros and cons of his positive views on the founders of Christianity, as Jews are traditionally reticent to discuss other religions, and especially Christianity. But considering the extreme puzzles associated with the Dead Sea Scrolls, and specifically the evidence that Jesus and Paul were acquainted with the Qumran sect—as many phrases from the Christian Bible seem to have been borrowed from the older Scrolls—I would wonder whether R. Emden's thesis might not serve as a key to unravel the mystery.

The majority of the scholarly community agrees that the Qumran sect were members of the Essenes (also known as Hasidim or *Tze'nuim* in Talmudic literature). No doubt can be entertained that the Essenes were extremely observant of the halakha, and no evidence of basic Christological beliefs has been found in the Scrolls.

Wouldn't it therefore be quite logical to assume that the opening paragraph of the Manual of Discipline, giving the *raison d'être* of the sect as "to do what is good and upright . . . as He has commanded through Moses," would also include spreading the knowledge of the Noahide Commandments to the Gentiles, as commanded by Moses? And when they further wrote "to love all the sons of light . . ." wouldn't that have included Gentiles who observed the Noahide Laws? I am not, however, insinuating that Jesus or Paul acted directly in collaboration with the Essenes or any other body.

In his letter to the Council of the Four Lands, Rabbi Emden, in what might be construed as a prophetic statement by a German rabbi rather than a literary slip, urges Christians to help Jews observe the Torah, as "commanded to you by your first teachers." He does not mention the names of Jesus and Paul here, but goes on to assure Christians that doing so will bring them reward and blessing. Could this rabbinic giant have sensed—two hundred years prior to the discovery of the Scrolls—that a group of pious Jews some two thousand years ago had sought to help their brethren observe the Torah during the coming exile by making Gentiles aware of its eternal binding character upon the Israelites? The Essenes, like the rest of the rabbinic community, knew from the prophecy of Daniel (9:24; cf. Nazir 32b) that the Second Temple was doomed to destruction in 70 C.E. They would have surely endeavored feverishly to complete their set goals, and prepare for the coming exile.

We shall in fact seek to present Talmudic evidence later in this book that the School of Hillel joined the Essenes in this mission to the Gentiles (see Chapter 3). We might then note here that a well-known statement of Hillel's now takes on new meaning. The sage states (Avot 1:12), "Be thou of the disciples of Aaron, one who loves peace, pursues peace, loves mankind, and draws them nigh to the Torah."

It is quite possible that Hillel was alluding here to a movement to spread knowledge of the Noahide Commandments to all mankind.

Returning now to the original statement of Hillel discussed in this chapter, it should be noted that Christian scholars have criticized what is generally believed to be Hillel's summation of the essence of Judaism as "What is hateful unto thee, do not unto thy neighbor," by comparing it to the positive statement of Jesus, "Whatsoever ye would that men should do unto you, even so do ye also unto them" (Matthew 7).

This criticism is resolved, as we now understand Hillel's statement not as the essence of Judaism, but of the Noahide Laws relating to Gentiles.

The two seemingly opposing statements may be placed in proper perspective by reviewing two important findings mentioned earlier. The first is Rabbi Jacob Emden's thesis that the founder of Christianity intended to bring personal salvation to the Gentiles through observance of the Noahide Laws. The second is the evidence from the Dead Sea Scrolls that Jesus was familiar with the Essenes and their writings, and wished to incorporate the spirit of the sect into his teachings. The Essenes were known as Hasidim, and the basic thrust of Hasidism in Judaism has always been understood as doing more than required by the Torah. (See *Mishnah* of the *Hasidim,* Jerusalem Talmud, Terumot 8:10; Measure of the Hasidim, Bava Mezia 52b, and *Lifnim Mi-shurat Hadin,* Bava Kamma 100a.)

We may now comprehend the two statements. Hillel informed the heathen what the Torah expects of him as an observant Noahide; a rabbi teaches the requirements of the Law, and the individual may elect to go beyond it. The founder of Christianity wished his followers to be "Hasidim of the Nations" in the literal sense of the word, by doing even more than required by the letter of the Noahide Laws, and therefore issued his positive exhortation.

(This has been the cause of a great deal of misunderstanding over the past two thousand years. Jesus spoke often about Judaism, but at other times about the Noahide Laws.[18] And regardless of which, he spoke at times according to the letter of the Law, and on other occasions in the spirit of Hasidism, or beyond the letter of the Law. This has caused much confusion.)

Hillel, Hasid and humble man, disciple of Ezra (Sanhedrin 11a), has thus laid the halakhic groundwork for the salvation of all mankind.

RABBINIC JUDAISM FACES TRINITARIANISM

I should stress again that the main goal of this book is to promote the concept that Jews and Christians will be more true and loyal to their respective faiths when they exhibit love and respect for one another's beliefs and traditions. In truth, rabbinic sources are traditionally reticent to discuss or pass judgment on other religions, except in cases of outright idolatry. Reliable, uncensored texts have also posed a problem.

The Tosafists, whose schools were spread throughout Christian Europe, ruled that Trinitarianism is not to be considered an idolatrous practice if adhered to by a Gentile, whereas it would be so if practiced by a Jew (Tosafists, Bekhorot 2b and Sanhedrin 63b).

The above opinion was rendered by R. Jacob Tam—outstanding twelfth century Tosafist and grandson of Rashi—when a question arose as to whether a Jew is permitted to cause a Christian to take an oath as a result of a business partnership, since he might cause the Christian to trespass the Noahide ban on idolatry. R. Tam's view that *Shittuf* (belief in God the Father, along with an additional deity) is permitted to Gentiles was accepted by the halakhist R. Moses Isserles (*Rema, Orah Hayyim* 156:1) and later authorities as well.[19]

This same R. Jacob Tam also expressed his belief that Peter (Simon Caiaphas), the first Pope, was a devout and learned Jew, who dedicated his life to guiding Christians along the proper path. R. Tam further maintained that Peter was the author of the *Nishmat* prayer recited on Sabbaths and Festivals, as well as a prayer for Yom Kippur (*Mahzor Vitry*, edited by S. Hurwitz, 1923, p. 285 note 5 and p. 362 note 5. Cf. J. Eisenstein's articles on Simon Caiaphas in *Otzar Israel* and *Otzar Midrashim*). It may also be noted that R. Judah He-Hasid, leader of the twelfth century Hasidei Ashkenaz in Germany, also referred to Peter as a pious man ("*zaddik*"; *Sefer Hasidim*, no. 191).

Traditional Christians believe in the divinity of Jesus, and many have even sought to convert Jews to this belief. In this regard, however, I find it important to note that I find Jesus asking Jews to believe in him as the Son of God on only two occasions—once when healing a blind man (John 9:35), and again before raising Lazarus from the dead (John 11:26). A blind man was considered by the Talmud to be the equivalent of a dead person, and this had halakhic implications (Nedarim 64b, 7b and cf. Bava Kamma 87a where the second century R. Judah declares a blind person to be exempt from all commandments of the Torah). I believe then that Jesus may be introducing an halakhic concept here, namely, that *Shittuf* (Trinitarianism) is permitted in order to save a Jewish life. For although the Talmud (Sanhedrin 74a) rules that a Jew must give his life rather than practice idolatry (murder and incest as well), Jesus would have interpreted this to apply to actual idolatry only, and not to *Shittuf*. That *Shittuf* is not actual idolatry—or is at least a lesser form of it—is evident from the fact that it is permitted to Gentiles, despite the Noahide ban on idolatry.

At the same time, it must be recognized that even some Christians do not interpret Jesus' references to himself as Son of God, as an allusion to his divinity.

In Talmudic literature, Noahides are always referred to as individuals, rather than as members of any organized religion. It was the individual Gentile's beliefs and behavior that evidently mattered to them. This is best reflected in the dialogue (Avodah Zarah 10b) between R. Judah Ha-Nasi and Antoninus: To the Roman's query as to whether he would merit the World to Come, the sage replied that he—or any Gentile—would, provided he did not practice "the deeds of Esau." (Cf. *Tiferet Israel*, Avot, Chap. 3—*Boaz*, Note 1.)

NOTES

1. See Maimonides, *Yad, Issurei Biah* 13:14–16.
2. Proverbs 27:10.
3. R. Samuel Eliezer Edels (*Maharsha*) derives from Hillel that love thy neighbor is not to be understood in the more stringent pos-

itive form, i.e., as mandating the granting of difficult favors, but is binding only in its negative sense, as in the context of the remainder of the verse, forbidding vengeance.

    R. Zevi Hirsch Chajes (*Maharitz Chayyes*) contends that Hillel was halakhically alluding to the fact that where self-preservation is involved, one's own life takes precedence over his neighbor's, as in Bava Mezia 62a.

4. Leviticus 25:35, Avodah Zarah 64b. Cf. Maimonides, *Issurei Biah* 14:7, *Avodat Kochavim* 10:6.

5. Sanhedrin 105a, 56a–59b; Rosh Ha-Shanah 17a; Maimonides, *Melakhim* Chap. 8–10.

6. Selling land or a house in Eretz Israel to an idolator was similarly forbidden by Maimonides (*Avodat Kochavim* 10:3–4). Fundamental contemporary halakhic problems pertaining to Israel involve these rules, such as selling the land to a non-Jew during the sabbatical year so that a Jew may work it.

7. Scholars have expressed puzzlement toward Hillel's use of the negative form. Our interpretation solves this, as the Noahide rules were indeed to be understood as negative Commandments (Sanhedrin 58b, bottom line).

8. Shabbat 130b and Tosafists ad loc.; Jerusalem Talmud, Betsah 1:4.

9. Bava Mezia 59b.

10. Sukkah 28a, Ta'anit 25b. R. Eliezer's teacher had been R. Johanan Ben Zakkai, who had received the tradition from both Hillel and Shammai (Avot 2:8). We shall later demonstrate (see Chapter 6) that R. Eliezer meant to say that he accepted and taught only those teachings transmitted in the name of Shammai.

11. Sanhedrin 105a. It is clear from the Talmudic text that R. Eliezer denied all Gentiles—even the righteous among them—a share in the World to Come. Some have found it difficult to accept that a leading first century rabbi should adopt such an unfair view. I have discussed this text with many scholars, and all agree that R. Eliezer denied salvation to all Gentiles. That R. Eliezer held this view is also manifest in Rashi's interpretation of R. Joshua's opposing statement (see Rashi's quotes from San-

hedrin 91b and Isaiah 61); R. Joseph Caro's notes in his commentary *Kesef Mishnah* to Maimonides (*Melakhim* 8:11, *Teshuvah* 3:5), as well as the clearer text of the Tosefta (Sanhedrin, Ch. 13).

The Soncino editor does initially attempt to force a new interpretation of R. Eliezer, whereby he would agree to the salvation of some Gentiles, but this editor himself deserts this position two footnotes later. It is understandable that the Soncino editor, translating the Talmud into English for the first time, was initially reticent to acknowledge R. Eliezer's true view.

12. Rabbi Eliezer is recorded as having harbored strong reservations on the acceptance of proselytes (Bava Mezia 59b). These, and other statements of his, reveal a deep distrust, if not hatred, of the pagan world. Shammai appears to have shared a similar view.

It would be difficult, however, to assume that R. Eliezer and Shammai were adverse to receiving the *Ger Toshav* as well as the *Ger Tzedek*.

See also the Talmudic discussion of Bet Hillel and Bet Shammai regarding divine reward and punishment in the afterlife (Rosh Ha-Shanah 16b–17a), where Bet Hillel specifically speaks of the salvation of Jews and Gentiles, whereas Bet Shammai makes no reference to Gentiles.

13. It should be stressed that even if one insists on understanding Shammai's use of the measuring rod in the usual literal sense, it would not detract from my new interpretation of Hillel.

14. The Talmud states (Arakhin 32b) that Jeremiah returned the exiled tribes to the land and Josiah reigned over them.

15. It is surprising that *Kesef Mishnah* and other later halakhists do not take note of this indirect but nevertheless explicit ruling of Rashi.

16. According to these three authorities, it should follow that the *Ger Toshav* was still formally accepted before three learned men during the Second Temple period. Even if not, the candidate would have surely had to appear before some rabbinic authority to receive permission to settle.

17. *Minhat Hinnukh*'s interpretation of Maimonides would not only

disalign the authority from the views of Rabad and Rashi, but seems to disregard the sage's usual reference to the rationale behind the halakha (as in *Avodat Kochavim* 10:4).

18. This book will address other statements of Jesus contained in the Gospels, which have been interpreted as critical of Jews and Judaism. We shall demonstrate how they were actually directed against Bet Shammai and their followers, who controlled Jewish life and thought in Jesus' time.

    One example would be Jesus' statement to his disciples (Matthew 10:5) to preach "only to the lost sheep of Israel." We now understand that he wished his fellow Jews to accept Bet Hillel's view that Gentiles too merit salvation. We shall later demonstrate that much Jewish suffering could have been avoided—including the Temple's destruction in the first century—had the Shammaites abandoned their hatred of the outside world. Yet another example would be Jesus' statement to his disciples following his death to "Make disciples of all the Gentiles" (Matthew 28:19). Some Christian scholars—such as Dr. Daniel Harrington (*Catholic Biblical Quarterly* 37 [1975] 359–369)—have insisted this means to the Gentiles only. But here again Jesus is only negating the views of Bet Shammai, while actually confirming Bet Hillel's position that the Gentile world too merits salvation.

19. It is difficult to ascertain Maimonides' view on this subject, as a passage relating to it has been altered in various editions (*Yad, Ma'akhalot Asurot* 11:7). The *Talmudic Encyclopedia* also omits reference to Maimonides on this issue (see *Ben Noah*, 1981 edition, 3:350).

3.

TALMUD AND JEWISH TRADITION ON THE ESSENES: RELATIONSHIP OF THE ESSENES TO BET HILLEL

It is difficult to theorize about the Essenes. This is so not only because they disappeared from sight some nineteen hundred years ago, but also because it was a secretive organization even in the zenith of its time. One of the awesome oaths taken by a member upon initiation to the sect after a probationary period was to never divulge a secret of the group to outsiders, even if tortured to death.[1] The Talmudic sages, their contemporaries, rarely mentioned them—and then only in veiled references.[2]

Shortly before the founding of the State of Israel, certain of their Scrolls were found near the Dead Sea. This will certainly help enrich our knowledge of their doctrine and activities. But even prior to the discovery, we possessed some knowledge of them from reliable ancient historians.[3] Trying to place the pieces together, a picture emerges of an extremely pious group of Jews, who cherished solitude, devotion and study, and expressed their love for God and mankind in their writings. Kaufmann Kohler, in what is probably the most comprehensive and readily accessible work on the subject (*Jewish Encyclopedia* 5:224)—based largely on Zacharias Frankel's earlier important writings—describes them as "a branch of the Pharisees who conformed to the most rigid rules of Levitical purity while aspiring to the highest degree

39

of holiness . . . in order to be initiated into the highest mysteries of heaven and cause the expected Messianic time to come." His description of them as a "branch of the Pharisees" has evidently been accepted by the more contemporary *Encyclopedia Judaica* (6:900), written after the Scrolls' discovery.

According to Kohler, wherever we find certain key phrases in Mishnah or Talmud, they must be examined as possible references to the Essenes. These would include: *Hasidim* (pious ones), *Zenu'im* (chaste ones), *Anav* (humble one), *Kesherim* (blameless ones), *Hashsha'im* (silent ones),[4] *Watikim* (men of firm principles), *Kadosh* (saint), *Banna'im* (builders), *Anshe Ma'aseh* (men of miraculous deeds). (References to *Hasidim*, *Zenu'im* and *Anav* appear often with grammatical variations in the Manual of Discipline.)

We know from Josephus that some of the Essenes were believed to possess prophetic powers, and most of them probably aspired to attain such a state. This would explain their abstinence from sexual relations, as was the case with Moses (Shabbat 87A), and Eldad and Medad who prophesied in his time.[5] Philo describes the Essenes as older men, who probably married and raised their children before joining the sect.[6]

A typical Talmudic text which might be affected by Kohler's thesis relates that secret names of God were entrusted only to the Tzanua and Anav of the priesthood (Kiddushin 71A). Were these Essenes? We know from the scrolls that there were many priests (*Kohanim*) in the Qumran community. If we assume that the Dead Sea Essenes were entrusted with Temple secrets, we may gain a better understanding of the mysterious Copper Scroll. According to it, the Essenes, shortly before the Temple's destruction in 70 C.E., were given vast Temple treasures to conceal. Only such as they would be entrusted with such knowledge.

We know that the sect existed for several centuries B.C.E. until about the time of the Second Temple's destruction. In the last chapter we expressed the view that the many similar phrases found in both the older Scrolls and the Christian Bible support the contention that the Essenes had a hand in the founding of Christianity. This would be best understood by the discussions of the Talmud (Sanhedrin 57A) and Maimonides (*Melakhim,* Ch. 8), indicating that Moses obligated the Jews to spread knowledge of the Noahide Commandments to all mankind.[7] The halakha states that Gentiles who observe these commandments are to be considered among the Hasidim of the Nations, and merit a share in the World to Come. We quoted from the writings of Rabbi Jacob Emden, who expressed the view that the original intent of Jesus and Paul was to bring salvation to the Gentiles through observance of the seven Noahide Commandments,[8] while the Jews should continue their adherence to Judaism (*Sefer Shimmush* and appendix to *Seder Olam*). (The first two of the Noahide Commandments, forbidding idolatry and blasphemy to Gentiles, are mentioned in the Damascus or "Zadokite" Document.)

The purpose of this chapter—bearing in mind that the Essenes were evidently "a branch of the Pharisees"—will be to determine whether some of the Pharisees (*Perushim*) mentioned in the Talmud might be identified as having also been members of the Essene Hasidim.[9] We shall also try to ascertain the views of the later Amoraim of the Talmud toward the Essenes, especially after the Church grew stronger and began exhibiting anti-Jewish tendencies. (Needless to say, an essay of this type must be brief, and we would hope to expand on it at some future time.)

It would appear that Kohler overshot the mark in certain areas. His depiction of Jose ben Joezer as an Essene has been accepted by many scholars, based on the Mishnah's identification of him as "Hasid of the Priesthood" (Hagigah 18B). However, R. Phinehas ben Jair's famous Baraita (Avodah

Zarah 20B), listing Hasidism (usually understood as religious activity above and beyond the requirements of the Torah) as the ultimate of the degrees leading to spiritual perfection, is not a valid reason to list him as an Essene. Hasidism can be practiced on an individual basis too—and certainly need not be understood in an organizational sense, as was the case with the Essenes.[10] R. Moshe Hayyim Luzzatto's eighteenth century ethical classic, *Mesillat Yesharim,*[11] which is based on the Baraita, was surely written for individual use. (Luzzatto's definitions of Pharisaism and Hasidism will be referred to later in the chapter.)

As in most cases involving esoteric matters, the sages of the Talmud spoke in vague terms.

The Benediction Against The Minim Was Directed
Against Jewish-Christians Only And Not Gentile Christians

Talmud, Berakhot 28B. "Rabban Gamaliel[12] said to the Sages: 'Can anyone among you compose a benediction relating to the Minim (Jewish Christians)?' Samuel the Little arose and composed it."

Question: All that was apparently involved here was to insert several words concerning the Minim into the *Amidah.* Couldn't any of the Sages have done it?[13] And why couldn't R. Gamaliel have composed it himself?

In order to answer this query, we shall have to delve further into the background of Samuel the Little, a disciple of Hillel who lived during the early part of the first century C.E.

Samuel the Little is mentioned twice on one folio of the Talmud, Sanhedrin 11A. I believe that a careful analysis of this source will provide us with important information concerning his possible affiliation with the Essenes. (Cf. Jerusalem Talmud, Sanhedrin 1:2, where R. Gamaliel compares him with Eldad and Medad.)

The Talmud first relates how he was willing to endure undeserved humiliation in order to spare embarrassment to another person. (We sense immediately his humility and concern for others, a trait which appears to have been shared by the members of the School of Hillel and the Essenes.) The text then cites similar acts by scholars of other periods, who learned to act in this manner from sages of earlier times. Thus, Samuel learned it from Shecaniah, son of Jehiel, a priest of Ezra's time, who in turn became aware of it from Joshua or Moses; R. Meir later learned it from Samuel, and R. Hiyya emulated R. Meir.

Before analyzing the Talmudic text further, it is worth noting some questions raised here by later commentaries. R. Solomon Luria (*Maharshal*) notes that the circumstances are not exactly the same in all the mentioned incidents—although all do allude to superior moral character with regard to others—and he also asks why it was necessary to name all these sages, since Samuel and the others could have learned it directly from Moses or Joshua. R. Samuel Edels (*Maharsha*) asks further why it was necessary for the Talmud to mention that each sage learned it from an earlier one; why couldn't each have acted on his own?

Before attempting a reply, we should complete our overview of the remainder of the Talmudic text concerning Samuel the Little.

The Talmud states that a *Bat Kol* (heavenly voice) was heard (on two separate occasions) declaring that Hillel and Samuel were worthy that the *Shekhinah* (Divine Presence) should rest upon them. When Hillel died, the Sages called him *Hasid* (pious man), *Anav* (humble man), disciple of Ezra. When Samuel the Little died, they called him *Hasid, Anav,* disciple of Hillel. Shortly before Samuel's death, he prophesied "Simeon and Ishmael will die by the sword, his friends will be executed, the rest of the people will be plundered, and many troubles will come upon the world."[14] They also wished to call R. Judah ben Bava *Hasid* and *Anav* after his death, but martyrs were not eulogized (for fear of the Romans).

Some additional issues should be noted regarding this portion of the text. To the best of my knowledge—and I have checked with others—no other sage aside from Samuel the Little is ever quoted in the Talmud as having made a major prophecy. It is also worth noting that Hillel, Samuel and R. Judah were not referred to as *Hasid* and *Anav* during their lifetimes, but only after their deaths.[15]

I realize the serious nature of what I am about to propose—especially with regard to Hillel, probably the most important and beloved sage of the Mishnah—but I write it after much study and soul-searching. I believe that Hillel, Samuel the Little, and R. Judah ben Bava were secretly members of the Essenes, at the same time they taught, or were members of, the Schools of the Pharisees. We must recall our earlier premise which considers the Essenes as "a branch of the Pharisees"; also Kohler's reference to Hasid and Anav as two of the most frequent titles assigned to Pharisees who were Essenes; also the fact that Essenes were noted for the accuracy of their prophecies. The necessity for the secrecy of their membership could be attributed to several accounts.[16] The description of Hillel as a disciple of Ezra, which must be symbolic since Ezra lived several centuries earlier, might be enhanced further by the thesis of some Dead Sea Scroll scholars that Ezra was the first Teacher of Righteousness (*Moreh Tzedek*) of the Essenes.[17]

We should in fact note that Hillel does not appear to have been a well-known member of the Pharisees at the time he was appointed *Nasi*. The discussion of the Talmud (Pesahim 66A) would seem to indicate that the sons of Bathyra, the previous holders of the office, hadn't heard of him. His subsequent re-

mark to them, almost blaming his appointment on their lack
of diligent study, demonstrates that he did not really seek the
office. (Cf. his statement, Avot 2:5, Where there are no men,
strive to be a man.)

Also worthy of note is his remark (Berakhot 63A) that
where others are available to teach the Torah, one should
keep to himself and not try to compete. In the Jerusalem Talmud (end Berakhot), this surprising statement is followed almost immediately by Resh Lakish's observation that a scroll of
the (Essene) Hasidim was found which emphasized constant
devotion.

Cf. Jerusalem Talmud, Nedarim, end Ch. 5, where Hillel
prophesies R. Johanan ben Zakkai's future as *Nasi* (as per *Karban ha-Edah*).

Returning now to the earlier portion of the text, we realize that every name mentioned there had some connection
with the Essenes—either before, during, or following its
known period of existence: Philo has described Moses as having trained thousands of disciples as Essenes.[18] (Interestingly,
both *Maharshal* and *Maharsha* have pointed out that it was actually God who refused to embarrass or accuse the true guilty
ones[19] in the cases attributed to Moses and Joshua.) Shecaniah
is quoted as speaking to Ezra,[20] and was probably one of the
first Essene priests. Kohler has noted that the *Kehilla Kaddisha
de-vi-Yrushalayim* (Holy Congregation in Jerusalem) probably
included remnants of the Essene community, and this group
was led by R. Meir's students;[21] R. Meir, a Tanna during the
second century C.E., was extremely meticulous concerning
the rules of levitical purity adhered to by the *Haverim* of the
Pharisees.[22] R. Hiyya, Tanna-Amora at the close of the second century C.E., was known to practice Hasidism,[23] and the
Megillat Setarim (secret scrolls) he possessed are considered by
Kohler to have contained Essene teachings.

The editor of the Soncino Talmud (Shabbat 6B) in fact cites other scholarly opinion to support the view that R. Hiyya's *Megillat Setarim* contained esoteric teachings. Although Rashi offers a different interpretation, it is possible the scrolls contained various types of material not meant for public dissemination.

It might be noted that the teachings of the *Megillat Setarim* both in Shabbat 6B and Bava Mezia 92A are given in the name of Issi ben Judah, whose identity is not clear. According to a Baraita (Pesahim 113B), four sages named Issi (including ben Judah) and two named Joseph were to be identified with Issi ben Akabia. The Jerusalem Talmud (Bava Kamma 3:7) further links him with Yose Kittunta, whom the Mishnah refers to as the last (important member) of the Hasidim (Sotah 49A).

It would seem to me that the literal resemblance of Issi to *Issi'im* (plural for Essenes) is too close to be ignored. I would therefore suggest that Issi ben Judah was an Essene, and their preference for anonymity is probably in line with Hillel's teaching (Avot 1:13), "A name made great is a name destroyed."

Hidden Scrolls Mentioned in the Talmud

R. Zevi Hirsch Chajes (*Maharitz Chayyes:* Shabbat 6B) writes that wherever the term "I found" is utilized in the Talmud, it refers to scrolls which were hidden from public view. Among these he lists the scholars' Book of Aggada (*Sefer Agad'ta D'bei Rav*) found by R. Jacob, containing rulings on the Noahide Laws (Sanhedrin 57B), the *Megilat Yuhasin* (genealogical scroll) found by ben Azzai (Yevamot 49A), and the Scroll of the (Essene) Hasidim found by Resh Lakish.

Of particular interest to this chapter is the scholars' Book of Aggada, which the Soncino editor describes according to Weiss (*Dor*) as a special scroll containing the set of Noahide laws relating to the Gentiles.

It may be noted that R. Judah ha-Nasi did not include the Noahide Laws in the Mishnah, which he edited about the beginning of the third century C.E. The earliest mention of them appears in the later Tosefta (Avodah Zarah, Ch. 9). Since these laws are based on Scripture and were discussed by earlier Tanna'im, it is difficult to understand why he omitted them.

That they are part and parcel of the Tradition from Sinai is evidenced by the fact that they are discussed in Tosefta, Talmud and Maimonides. If there was any fear of a harsh reaction from the Gentiles to the Jews' possession of a set of rules meant for them, it would have surely been omitted from the later works as well. I have discussed this omission with several scholars, and they too were at a loss to explain it. If we adopt R. Jacob Emden's thesis that Jesus and Paul founded Christianity on the Noahide Laws, it might be reasoned that public knowledge of these rules would have weakened Christianity. (R. Jacob Emden alludes to this in *Sefer Shimmush*.) The Rabbis therefore waited until they saw Christianity grow strong before publishing the Noahide Laws.

This would explain why the traditional account concerning the heathen who appeared before Hillel to learn the Torah while standing on one foot (we have earlier explained it as a reference to the Noahide Commandments) does not mention the Noahide rules explicitly; nor does the one-footed convert appear alongside the other two (of Shabbat 31A) in the earlier Avot D'Rabbi Nathan (Ch. 15).

This assumption would also explain why Jesus and Paul did not mention the Noahide rules explicitly. It might be noted however that the first Gentiles admitted to the Mother

Church in Jerusalem under Paul's insistence were accepted
on condition they observe the prohibitions against pollutions
of idols, fornication, things strangled, and blood (Acts 15),
which are an early Tannaitic variant of the Noahide laws
found in Tosefta Avodah Zarah 9:4. This fact did not escape
R. Emden's scrutinizing eye.

This interpretation of the Talmud might serve as a reply
to the aforementioned questions raised by *Maharshal* and *Maharsha*. The basic purpose of the Talmud here was to stress
the exemplary moral character of the Biblical and Talmudic
personalities connected in one way or another with the Essene
Hasidim and their reliance on tradition.

Returning now to our original question—as to why R.
Gamaliel couldn't have chosen any sage to compose the benediction against the Jewish-Christians—we may now comprehend R. Gamaliel's question and the ethical problem he faced
in a much clearer manner.

One may ask why the benediction was to only include the
Minim; why not Gentile Christians?[24] And why not Jesus of
Nazareth, who had established the new faith? However, R.
Gamaliel surely knew—having been Hillel's grandson, and
the teacher of Paul of Tarsus as well—of Jesus' involvement
with the Essenes. He surely knew that Jesus had meant to establish a religion for the Gentiles, so that they might achieve
salvation through observance of the Noahide Commandments. He knew that the establishment of Christianity as a
Gentile religion was, as R. Jacob Emden points out in his letter
to the Council of the Four Lands, entirely according to the
Halakha ("*hakol al pi din v'dat Toratenu*" or "all according to the
law and custom of our Torah"). It was therefore necessary
that the composer be an Essene, one who had sat in on the sessions at the caves of Qumran, and who knew as a first-hand
witness the true chain of events. Samuel the Little then arose,
and composed the benediction.

A Mission to the Gentiles by the Essenes and Bet Hillel

Talmud, Sukkah 28A: "Hillel the Elder had 80 disciples, 30 of whom were worthy of the Divine Spirit resting upon them . . . 30 of whom were worthy that the sun should stand still for them. . . . The greatest of them was Jonathan ben Uzziel, the smallest of them was Johanan ben Zakkai. . . ."

Jerusalem Talmud (Nedarim, end Ch. 5): "Hillel the Elder had 80 pairs of disciples. . . ."

Question: Why was R. Johanan ben Zakkai appointed *Nasi*—rather than one of the other 79, who were greater than he?[25] And what became of the remaining 79?

Question: There seems to be a conflict here between the Babylonian and Jerusalem Talmuds as to whether Hillel had 80 or 160 disciples!

For a proper reply to these queries, I believe we must turn to Hagigah 16A, where the Mishnah speaks of the first dispute that arose among the sages of Israel: it deals with the issue of whether the laying on of hands (on the head of a sacrifice) was permitted on a festival. Four succeeding pairs of *Nasi* (President of the Sanhedrin) and *Av-Bet-Din* (Vice-President of the Sanhedrin) disagreed, but Hillel and Menahem did not differ.[26] Menahem went forth, Shammai entered (in his place). Hillel and Shammai then disagreed.

R. Jehiel Heilprin (*Seder Ha-Dorot* 2:271) identifies this Menahem, who first served with Hillel, as Menahem the Essene—whom Herod was fond of for having prophesied his rise to power. Such modern scholars as Kaufmann Kohler[27] and Louis Ginzberg[28] agreed with this identification.

The Talmud to this Mishnah asks what actually happened to Menahem. Abbaye and Rava—two Amoraim who lived during the fourth century C.E.—disagreed concerning this. Abbaye claimed that Menahem went forth into evil ways; Rava states he went forth to the King's service. The Talmud brings a baraita to support Rava's view, where it is stated that Menahem went forth to the King's service, along with 80 pairs of disciples dressed in silk.

This dispute among the later Talmudic authorities over what happened to Menahem—probably about 20 B.C.E.—is also cited in the Jerusalem Talmud (Hagigah 2:2), albeit anonymously and with added detail.[29] The first opinion describes Menahem as having left the Pharisees to join a conflicting religious group (the Essenes), which only reiterates Abbaye's negative stance toward Menahem—and the Essenes as well. To Rava's view is added a postscript explaining that Menahem was forced to leave because the Gentiles were coercing (or would soon coerce?) the Jews to abandon their religious beliefs, and he and the 80 pairs of disciples left to remedy this. Rava thus adopts a positive view of Menahem's departure, which according to R. David Fraenkel (*Karban ha-Edah*), was a mission to reconcile or appease "the nations." (It should be noted here that in scores of disputes between Rava and Abbaye in the Talmud, the view of the former is always— with six specific exceptions—accepted.)

We of course recognize that we are dealing here with an historic-philosophic dispute between Rava and Abbaye, and not one concerning a specific halakha. Also, Rava's statement concerning achieving a reconciliation with the Gentiles calls for further elucidation, as we do not recall mention of such a mission elsewhere.[30]

Returning now to the Baraita of R. Phineas ben Jair mentioned at the beginning of this chapter, we recall that Hasidism was listed as a higher degree of spiritual attainment than Pharisaism; yet the sources would seem to indicate that most Talmudic sages did not practice Hasidism—whether on an individual basis or in an organized state, such as the Essenes did. R. Moshe Hayyim Luzzatto, in his classic, *Mesillat Yesharim* (Ch. 13), explains that both Pharisaism and Hasidism involve observance of the Torah beyond the letter of the law, [31] and Pharisaism is also referred to as "Mishnah of the Hasidim," praised by the Prophet Elijah. However, while Pharisaism in the main denotes abstinence and "building fences," which is the first phase of Hasidism, Hasidism itself demands more positive action.[32] We might also note here that Rava is mentioned several times by Luzzatto as one who practiced Hasidism.[33]

Abbaye's negative outlook toward the Essenes and Hasidism might be understood in light of his remark (Berakhot 45A), "Go forth and see how the public are accustomed to act," in concert with Hillel's statement, "An ignorant man cannot be a Hasid" (Avot 2:5).[34] In other words, some religious leaders feared that Hasidism might cause a schism between the laity and the scholarly community. But Luzzatto cites an even greater danger inherent in Hasidism (Ch. 20)[35]— namely, that an action in itself may seem worthy enough of performance, but the results might prove harmful. He cites two examples. Gedaliah ben Ahikam, appointed Governor of Judah by the Babylonians, who—because of his Hasidism— refused to accept Johanan ben Kareach's warning concerning Ishmael ben Nathaniah's treacherous intentions (Jeremiah 40). As a result, Gedaliah was killed, the Jews' last hopes for independence at the time were dashed, and Jeremiah considered Gedaliah personally responsible for those murdered by Ishmael.[36] Luzzatto cites as another example the Talmud's condemnation of R. Zechariah ben Avkulot (Gittin 56A), whose act of Hasidism led to the Second Temple's destruction.[37] This is surely why Abbaye and many others shunned (and deprecated) acts of Hasidism which might ultimately cause harm to the people.

A careful reading of the Talmud (Sanhedrin 57A) and Maimonides (*Melakhim*, Ch. 8) would indicate that Moses obligated the Jews to spread knowledge of the Noahide Commandments to the Gentiles only from a position of strength, the potential dangers inherent toward the Jews by creating such a new religion among the Gentiles being only too apparent now after Crusades, inquisitions, pogroms and the Holocaust. Thus, according to the halakha, Moses' obligation never became operative—as the Jews never attained such a level of power and safety. It was only an act of Hasidism, above and beyond the letter of the law—motivated by love of God and fellow man—that caused the Essenes to originate and develop Christianity in line with the Noahide Laws passed down from Moses at Sinai (*Halakha L'Moshe mi-Sinai*. Cf. R. Emden's letter).

By the fourth century, the Church had grown strong, but also exhibited anti-Jewish tendencies. The Talmudic sages knew only too well of the Essenes' involvement, and this led to Abbaye's condemnation of Menahem the Essene and the sect in general.

Rava, the Hasid, tells us in a veiled statement (*Melitza*) that Menahem and the eighty pairs of disciples left for the "service of the King," by the "King" meaning God. It would seem that shortly before the turn of the common era, a conservative movement in Judaism, led by Shammai, began to gain considerable strength[38]—advocating more separation from the Gentiles, rather than less. This later led to passage of the eighteen measures (Shabbat 13B) by the School of Shammai, designed to cause more isolationism from the nations. (Was Menahem actually forced out by Shammai's group?)[39] Hillel and Menahem both believed in Hasidism, and were in fact Essenes. Menahem left the Pharisees with his own eighty disciples, and virtually all of Hillel's disciples as well, to lead the Essenes in establishing a religion for the Gentiles. (The reference to "dressed in linen" would be to the special cloak worn by the sect.) Rava, the Hasid, could not condemn the Essenes,[40] for they had meant well—both for Jews during the coming exile, and for Christians as well.[41]

We now understand what happened to Hillel's other disciples, they having joined the Essenes. The additional eighty disciples ascribed to him by the Jerusalem Talmud were actually those of Menahem.

Criticism of the Pharisees in the Dead Sea Scrolls

The criticism contained in the Damascus—or "Zadokite"—Document of the Dead Sea Scrolls against those who "build up a rickety wall . . ." is usually taken as an Essene criticism of the Pharisees. It would be particularly hazardous to attempt new interpretations here, since this Scroll not only seems to have undergone rescensions, but also appears to be an abridgement of a longer work.

However, since those criticized in the Scroll are described as marrying two wives simultaneously, and also as marrying their nieces, we may well identify them as members of Shammai's School, and not Bet Hillel. The Jerusalem Talmud relates (Yevamot 13:2) that R. Eliezer ben Hyrcanus married his niece in his later years (cf. Avot D'Rabbi Nathan, Ch. 16), and yet the Talmud states explicitly (Sanhedrin 68A) that his wife Imma Shalom, daughter of R. Simeon ben Gamaliel I, outlived him—thus demonstrating that he married two wives simultaneously, one of them his niece. R. Eliezer's position is described as never conflicting with that of Bet Shammai (Jerusalem Talmud, Betsah 1:4), as he was a member of their School; and since virtually no Talmudic sages ever practiced polygamy (cf. *Me'iri*, Ketubbot 62B), we may assume that the Damascus Document's condemnation was directed specifically against the School of Shammai.[42] Louis Ginzberg (*An Unknown Jewish Sect*) and C. Rabin (*Qumran Studies*) have both noted R. Eliezer's marriage to his niece, but failed to quote the Talmud in Sanhedrin proving that he practiced polygamy, and, more importantly, his centrality in ascertaining Bet Shammai's practice.

I would therefore suggest the following identities for the mysterious unnamed parties discussed in the Damascus Document: The "Expounder of the Torah" (*Doresh ha-Torah*) is Menahem, former *Av Bet Din* of the Pharisees; the "Babbling Preacher" (*matif*) and "Man of Lies" (*Ish ha-Kazav*) is Shammai, leader of an opposing group of Pharisees; the "Builders of a Rickety Wall" (*Bonai Haitz*) and "Men of War" (*Anshe Milhama*) are the School of Shammai, and would probably allude to a time when they had gained ascendancy over Bet Hillel; the "Princes" and "Nobles of the People" are the eighty pairs of disciples of Hillel and Menahem, who are described as having departed from the Land of Judah to sojourn in "the Land of Damascus" in order to search for God. They are further described as having entered a "new covenant," and living in encampments with their wives and children. This would have probably taken place about 20 B.C.E., and would therefore identify this scroll as having been written by the disciples of Menahem and Hillel, who joined the Essenes when the Shammaites gained control of the Pharisees.

(Cf. other chapters in this book where we have interpreted Jesus' criticism of the Pharisees as being directed specifically against Bet Shammai, and not Bet Hillel. Some of the language utilized by Jesus and the Essenes is notably similar.)

Similar descriptions in other scrolls, such as the *Pesher* (Commentary on) Habakkuk and *Pesher* Micah, would be understood in like vein. The "Preacher of Lies" (*Matif ha-Kazav*) and "Man of Lies" is Shammai; the "Traitors" (*Bogdim*) are Bet Shammai; while the "Teacher" (*Moreh*) might well be Menahem.

The difficult term "House of Absalom" (*Bet Avshalom*)

which appears in the Habakkuk Commentary appears to be an allusion to King David's son who rebelled against him. This might well be a reference to Bet Shammai who rebelled against the authority of Menahem and Hillel. However, a careful reading of the entire passage, and consideration of the fact that Hillel was a descendant of King David (Ketubbot 62B; Jerusalem Talmud, Ta'anit 4:2), would seem to suggest that the House of Absalom is the Sanhedrin who are censured for having allowed Shammai's rise to power. The Teacher (*Moreh Tzedek*) in this case might well have been Hillel.

These identifications will help explain a prophecy contained in the Damascus Document foretelling that about forty years will elapse from the death of the Teacher until the followers of the Man of Lies will come to an end; and at that time God's anger will be kindled against Israel. The Temple was destroyed in 70 C.E., and it was at about that time that the Heavenly Voice was heard in Yavneh proclaiming the halakha in favor of Bet Hillel. This would fix the Teacher's death at about 30 C.E. Any attempt, however, to connect this with Jesus' death would be foolhardy, as many others might have died that year, including Menahem.

This interpretation is particularly valid if we adopt the scholarly opinion that the Damascus Document was written by a special branch of the Qumran *Yahad* at a later time, and certainly if the reference to Damascus is not to be taken literally (cf. *Encyclopedia Judaica* 5:1248–1249).

We might also note that R. Judah he-Hasid, leader of the twelfth century German Hasidim (*Hasidei Ashkenaz*), expressly forbade marriage to a niece (*Sefer Hasidim, Tzava'ah,* #22), thus establishing a link between the Essenes and later Hasidim.

See also his *Sefer Hasidim* #358, that one should honor a Gentile who zealously observes the Noahide Commandments more than a Jew who doesn't occupy himself with the Torah.

M'kor Hesed bases this on R. Meir's teaching (Sanhedrin 59A) that a Gentile who studies the Noahide commandments is considered the equal of a High Priest.

The Beginnings of Bet Hillel and Bet Shammai

In order to place the beginnings of Bet Shammai and Bet Hillel in proper perspective, we might refer to Zacharias Frankel (*Darke Hamishnah* pp. 54–55) who proposed that—on the basis of the extreme passions displayed at the time—the first two controversies between the two Schools were over the "eighteen measures" (Shabbat 13B–17A) and the bringing of the Festival burnt-offering sacrifice on the first day of the Jewish holidays (Betsah 19A–20B). (The eighteen measures were a set of rulings advocated by Bet Shammai in order to foster greater separation between Jews and Gentiles, these rules being opposed by Bet Hillel. In the second case, Bet Shammai forbade the bringing of the festive burnt-offering at the Temple by individual Jews on the first day of the three major festivals, holding that they should be offered on later dates, whereas Bet Hillel ruled they should be brought on the first day.) Frankel further wrote that although the Talmud (Yevamot 14B) records that friendship and love existed between the two Schools, this would apply to later decades, and not to the beginnings of the two groups. He seems correct on both these assumptions.

It would seem then that about 20 B.C.E., when Shammai succeeded Menahem as *Av Bet Din* (Vice-President of the Sanhedrin), an attempt was made to keep peace between the two Schools. They would meet at the home of Hananiah ben Hezekiah—a sage who was devoting all his time to a major work on Ezekiel—who was revered by all for his dedication to scholarship (see Shabbat 13B). It was surely hoped that his influence would help keep the peace. (This Hananiah was a member of the leading family of the Zealot party, who advocated armed revolution against the Roman conquerors, hated the Gentile world, and had close ties to Bet Shammai, as we shall note later in this book. His father, Hezekiah, was the actual founder of the Zealots—Josephus called him a "chief bandit"—and was executed by Herod. Hananiah, however, was above politics, and devoted to pure scholarship.) At his home, the two schools collaborated in writing certain historical works together (see the eighth century C.E. Geonic work *Halakhot Gedolot, Hilkhot Soferim*).

The evidence suggests that the debate regarding the eighteen measures arose first. Before the vote was taken at Hananiah's home, the Jerusalem Talmud (Shabbat 1:4) tells us that an unspecified number of Bet Hillel were killed by Bet Shammai. Two versions of the incident are recorded, demonstrating that eyewitnesses later gave testimony regarding it. I would suggest—based on further evidence we shall soon refer to—that it was at this time that the disciples of Hillel left to join the Essenes. (I have previously written that the Damascus Document of the Dead Sea Scrolls was written by the disciples of Hillel and Menahem. Since it now appears that Hillel's disciples left a short time later than Menahem's group, it is possible that the Document was written by Menahem's disciples alone.)

I should like to suggest here—based on the writings of R. Saadiah Gaon, as well as another passage in the Jerusalem Talmud—that the Zealots committed the actual murders, and not Bet Shammai themselves. The evidence, however, is complex and involves other periods in Jewish history. (Cf. article on Bet Hillel in the *Jewish Encyclopedia*, which seems to concur with this view.) I also noted earlier that this Hananiah was a member of the leading Zealot family, and the Zealots were referred to as murderers by both the Talmud and Josephus. These Zealots were also known as *"sicarii"* or dagger-men, and both Talmuds refer to swords being present in the House of Study that day. Both Talmuds and the Tosefta also state that that day was as troublesome for Israel as the day the Golden Calf was built in Moses' time.

By the time the second debate between the two Schools arose concerning the Festival burnt-offering, it is evident from both Talmuds that Bet Shammai was completely in control. The Jerusalem Talmud notes (Betsah 2:4) that the Jerusalem Temple's courtyard was empty on the first day of the holidays, because all the people observed Bet Shammai's opinion. Bava ben Buta, himself a member of Bet Shammai, but holding the Halakha to be in favor of Bet Hillel in this case, said of his own school, "May their homes become desolate, for they have made desolate the House of our God." He then used his own great prestige to swing the vote in favor of Bet Hillel. His important standing may be gauged from the fact that Herod rebuilt the Temple at his counsel (Bava Batra 4A).

That Hillel's disciples had already left by this time is also evident from the fact that Shammai's students "ganged up" on Hillel as he brought his burnt-offering to the Temple in accordance with his School's opinion (Betsah 20A). It would appear that he was alone, and Shammai's disciples had the run of the grounds.

Scholars' Views on the Essenes

As this chapter draws to a close, we should note that scholars have expressed puzzlement for centuries over the fact that the Talmudic sages never made specific reference to the Essenes.

Isaac Hirsch Weiss, in his *Dor,* believed that the Rabbis disdained them so vehemently that they refrained from even mentioning them by name. However, such scholars as Zacharias Frankel, Derenbourg, Geiger and Kaufmann Kohler have expressed the view that the Sages referred to them by other titles, especially Hasidim—and on favorable terms. The discovery of the Dead Sea Scrolls in the Caves at Qumran— which the scholarly community has virtually unanimously identified as having belonged to the Essenes—actually proves the latter correct, as the Talmud specifically mentions a "Cave of the Hasidim" (Mo'ed Katan 17A), and quotes from a "Scroll of the Hasidim" (Jerusalem Talmud, end Berakhot). Weiss' theory is unacceptable on other grounds as well, as the Talmudic sages—with a penchant for truthfulness—grant sufficient space even to such known heretical movements as the Sadducees, Boethusians, Jewish-Christians, Philosophers, etc.

K. Kohler also maintained that Talmudic sages referred to as *Abba* (father) were Essenes. I believe that the Dead Sea Scrolls' criticism of the Jerusalem Temple's priests buttresses his position, as we find three Talmudic sages, Abba Saul, Abba Saul ben Batnit and Abba Joseph, denouncing the corruption of the priests and even High Priests of their time in most derisive terms (Pesahim 57A and Tosefta Menahot 13:21).

It is also interesting to note that R. Johanan ben Zakkai is quoted (Avot 2:8) as naming R. Eliezer as the greatest of his disciples. However, we find another tradition given there by Abba Saul, who quotes R. Johanan ben Zakkai as identifying R. Eleazar ben Arakh as his most distinguished disciple. We have already offered evidence that the Essenes had strong ties with Bet Hillel—especially as Hillel and others of his school were also known as Hasidim—and it would be quite understandable that Abba Saul, an Essene, would find it difficult to recognize R. Eliezer, a follower of Bet Shammai, as the greatest of the Nasi's disciples.

Earlier in this chapter, I also suggested that certain sages named Issi (singular for *Issi'im* or Essenes) were Essenes. This thesis is based primarily on a puzzling Talmudic passage (Pesahim 113B) which states that five sages named Issi and two by the title of Joseph were one and the same. Judah Eisenstein has already noted (*Otzar Israel,* Issi ben Akiva) that the passage cannot be taken literally, since we find Issi ben Judah and Issi ben Gur-Aryeh, two of those mentioned, debating one another in the Mekhilta. Our interpretation would therefore be that all were members of the same secretive Essene organization, who adopted the appellation upon joining the group. Support may be brought from the Talmud (Shabbat 6B) where Issi ben Judah is quoted in the *Megillat Setarim* (Secret Scrolls), which Kohler and others have identified as Essene scrolls.

See Sotah 15B, where Issi ben Judah and Issi ben Menahem dispute a point concerning the Temple; this too appears to be an Essene debate.

We have previously expressed our belief—based especially on the many similarities between the Christian Bible and the Dead Sea Scrolls—that the Essenes helped found Christianity as a religion for the Gentiles, in accordance with the Noahide Commandments. This view is based on the writings of the eighteenth century Talmudist and mystic, Rabbi Jacob Emden, who believed that Jesus established Christianity entirely according to the Halakha, as an observance of the Noahide Commandments. It is therefore worthy of note that it was Issi ben Akiva, an Essene sage, who taught that the biblical prohibition of murder applies to the lives of Jews and Gentiles alike (Mekhilta to Exodus 21:14). This teaching also appears in the Damascus Document of the Essenes. This would all be in line with the Essene creed "To love all the sons of light" (Manual of Discipline).

See also the perplexing statement of R. Assi (Niddah 36B), describing himself as "I am Issi ben Judah who is Issi ben Gur-Aryeh, etc." Our interpretation of Pesahim 113B would suggest that he is identifying himself here as an Essene. Cf. Rav advising R. Assi (Pesahim 113A) not to reside in a city whose leader is an "*Asya*," which Rashi explains as a physician or scholar; the reference is probably to an Essene. Rav was known as "Abba" Arikha, and was probably also an Essene.

Certain twentieth century scholars have interpreted the Scrolls of the Essenes as being anti-Pharisee in character because they contain criticism of the *Perushim* (Pharisees). They also base their view on the fact that a calendar was found in the caves which differs from that of normative Judaism, and occasional statements appear in the Scrolls which differ from Pharisaic tradition (i.e., the Temple Scroll mentions the *Omer* ceremony as taking place each year on the Sunday following the first day of Passover; see Menahot 65A).

With regard to the criticisms of Pharisees, this book will attempt to demonstrate that these are actually attacks on the School of Shammai by allies of Bet Hillel. The Talmud in fact mentions (Mo'ed Katan 17A) a "Cave of the Hasidim" and another "Cave of the Judges." It is most probable that the Hasidim were the Essenes themselves, whose guidelines were outlined in the Manual of Discipline; the "Judges" were the disciples of Hillel and Menahem who later joined the Essenes (as evidenced by Hagigah 16B, and see elsewhere in this chapter), their creed being spelled out in the Damascus Document, and the title "Judges" deriving from their previous connection with the Sanhedrin. The Talmud (Mo'ed Katan 17A) clearly considered the Essenes to be imbued with a higher degree of holiness than the judges. (Cf. R. Jacob Emden's *hiddushim* to Shabbat 10A where he interprets the term "Hasidim" differently than the Tosafists.)

As for the deviating halakhic statements or the calendar, it is important to note that Rashi (Shabbat 6B) maintains that the *Megillat Setarim* (Secret Scrolls)—for which we have

quoted scholarly opinion identifying them as Essene Scrolls—
contained minority views which would have been forgotten
had they not been committed to writing. The great commentator seems to be telling us that the Essenes recorded views
which were known to be at variance with the correct Pharisaic
tradition. Was their library some form of national archive?
(Other explanations may be advanced for these occasional
difficulties; I have drawn attention to the Rashi because I
have not seen anyone else take note of it.)

Our view of the Damascus Document corresponds with
that of Louis Ginzberg (see his *An Unknown Jewish Sect*) who
maintained—following its discovery in the Cairo Genizah—
that he saw nothing anti-Pharisee in it. Solomon Schechter
and others who believed that it was were probably influenced
by sheer puzzlement as to who was being criticized if not the
general Pharisee party.

NOTES

1. See *Jewish Encyclopedia* 5:229.
2. See "Cave of the Hasidim," Mo'ed Katan 17A; also, Resh Lakish, third century C.E. Talmudic sage, quotes from a scroll of
   the Hasidim which was found (Jerusalem Talmud, end Berakhot).
3. Josephus, Philo and Pliny among others.
4. Kohler believes this might be a reference to the Chamber of Secrets (Shekalim 5:6) in the Temple, where charity funds were
   deposited and taken in anonymity; the Essenes are described as
   collectors of funds for the needy.
   It may also allude to secret teachings which were given "in
   a whisper" (Hagigah 13A and 14A).
5. Josephus' writings concerning Essene prophecy can be found
   in *Jewish Encyclopedia*, pp. 224–225.
   Moses abstained from conjugal relations from the Reve-

lation at Sinai onward. Rashi (Numbers 12:1 from Sifre) quotes Tzipporah, wife of Moses, as expressing sorrow for the wives of Eldad and Medad—realizing that as prophets they would abstain from sexual relations.

6. *Jewish Encyclopedia* 5:228.

The remains of females and children found in the Qumran cemetery are surely those of family members.

7. Surprise must be expressed here toward scholarly neglect of the Noahide laws, and the important part they appear to have played in history. See for example Robert Travers Herford's piece on the Essenes in *Universal Jewish Encyclopedia* (1941), where he writes, "They may have done so (contributed to the origin and growth of the Church); but there is no positive evidence that they did, and no obvious reason why they should have." Perhaps we now have both the reason and the evidence.

8. The basic seven Noahide Commandments consist of the prohibitions against idolatry, blasphemy, killing, stealing, sexual sins, eating the limb of a living animal (kindness to animals), and the obligation to establish courts of justice.

9. R. Abraham Zacuto, in the introduction to his *Sefer ha-Yuhasin*, lists the following as Hasidim: Jose ben Joezer, R. Jose the Priest, R. Judah ben Bava, R. Judah bar Ilai, King David, Ezra the Priest, Hillel, Bava ben Buta, R. Akiva, Samuel the Little, Simeon he-Hasid. This listing is of course far from complete, and gives no hint as to which might have belonged to the Essenes.

10. Kohler's reference to Wilhelm Bacher in order to bolster his contention that R. Phinehas was an Essene seems in error; for although Bacher (*Aggadot Tanna'im* 2:2 159) does cite some scholarly sources as entertaining the idea, Bacher himself states that there is no basis for this. Bacher thus concurs with our position that no Tanna referred to as Hasid can be considered to have been an Essene unless some evidence from Talmudic sources can be cited to support the assumption.

In general, Kohler further identifies such Biblical figures as King Saul and his daughter (p. 226), Jesse, Boaz, all the way back to Abraham (p. 231), as types of Essenes. He seems to be confusing personal Hasidism with the organized Hasidism of the Essenes.

    (It might also be noted here that the Manual of Discipline begins by giving the purpose of the sect as to do what is "good and upright," an apparent reference to Deuteronomy 6:18. The Talmud (Bava Mezia 16B) interprets this verse as referring to action above and beyond the requirements of the Torah, especially with regard to one's fellow man.)

11. The best available translation to English is *The Path of the Just,* by Silverstein (Feldheim, 1966).

12. We shall see in note 14 that the Commentaries identify him as R. Gamaliel the Elder, grandson of Hillel, and not R. Gamaliel of Yavneh, great-great-grandson of Hillel.

13. This question has been raised by the Gaon R. Joseph B. Soloveitchik, and is also repeated in the name of R. Israel Salanter, father of the *Mussar* (ethical) movement in Judaism. Both have cited Samuel's teaching (Avot 4:19)—not to rejoice over the fall of an enemy (i.e., he bore no personal animosity toward them)—as the basis for his qualification.

14. Rashi (Sanhedrin 11A) identifies the Simeon in the prophecy as R. Simeon ben Gamaliel I, son of R. Gamaliel the Elder, and Ishmael as Ishmael ben Elisha, the High Priest.

    This has led later commentators to identify the Rabban Gamaliel who introduced the benediction against the Minim in Yavneh as R. Gamaliel the Elder; for if it were R. Gamaliel of Yavneh, how could Samuel have prophesied before his death concerning the martyrdom of his father, R. Simeon? The later R. Gamaliel would certainly not have acted as Nasi while his father still lived!

    This view is taken by R. Samuel Strashun (*Rashash*), and also by Aaron Hyman, *Toledot Tanna'im* (see Samuel the Little). The latter points out that the Minim were already causing turmoil in the time of R. Gamaliel the Elder (end Acts 5), and the rabbis were meeting regularly at Yavneh after 30 C.E.

    R. Jacob Emden appears to concur with them (see close of the first of his two remarks on the subject in his *Hiddushim* to Sanhedrin).

15. Cf. Berakhot 6B from where it is apparent that no one was called Hasid or Anav during the one's lifetime in the Talmudic era.

16. The Essenes seem to have always been a secretive sect. If we assume—as was probably so—that such leaders as Ezra and Jose ben Joezer, the first Nasi, were members, it was certainly without fanfare.

   If, as we believe, they also sought to establish a religion for the Gentiles, they would have certainly not sought public attention.

17. Theodor H. Gaster (*The Dead Sea Scriptures*, 1976, pp. 29 and 107) prefers Ezra to Nehemiah, as the Teacher is described to be a *Kohen; et al.*

18. *Jewish Encyclopedia*, p. 228.

19. Rabbinic sources advocate man's emulation of God's ways (Shabbat 133B).

   (Kohler believed that the title *Abba* [Father] referred to Essenes [*Encyclopedia Judaica* 2:31], and it is therefore worth noting that the above teaching is given in the name of Abba Saul.

   Scholars have noted that he is not usually mentioned together with other Tanna'im; that his terminology was different from that normally used; and that he appears to have possessed a different set of the Mishnah, which Judah ha-Nasi may have used.

   His mother's name was *Imma* [Mother] Miriam [Ketubbot 87A]. This implies that the titles *Abba* and *Imma* were frequently used in the circles of the Hasidim, and therefore has relevance to the fact that these appellations have been used among Christians.

   Abba Saul was also known as Son of Man [Niddah 25B], a title often referred to by Jesus of Nazareth.)

20. Ezra 10. (The *Yahad* originally consisted of three priests and twelve laymen.)

21. R. Meir was considered to be the spiritual father of this group (also known as the *Edah Kdoshah*), which was known to be particularly scrupulous with regard to levitical cleanliness. They divided their time between study, prayer and work.

Cf. C. Rabin, *Qumran Studies,* who devotes an entire chapter to the similarities between the two groups.

22. See Tosefta Demai, Chapters 2 and 3, and especially 2:8, where R. Meir rules that a Haver who leaves can never again be accepted. This has been found to correspond to a similar ruling of the Essenes in the Manual of Discipline (7:1).

> R. Meir also adopts the ethical spirit of Bet Hillel and the Essenes, as in Avot 6:1, where he describes the true Torah scholar as one who "loves mankind," and becomes a Hasid and Tzanua. R. Meir appears to have attempted a symbiosis of Pharisaism and Hasidism.

23. Bava Kamma 99B.

24. Cf. Reuven Kimmelman's essay in *Jewish and Christian Self-Definition* (Fortress, 1981; E.P. Sanders, editor). Any attempt to relate the benediction against the Minim to Gentile Christians would be a serious violation of Jewish scholarship and tradition.

25. R. Joseph Caro, in his commentary *Kesef Mishnah* to Maimonides (*Mamrim* 2:2), suggests that he was smallest in other branches of knowledge, but greatest in Torah. He himself, however, appears dubious of this. Rabad (*ibid.*) clearly assumes him to have been the least among Hillel's disciples. Philip Blackman (*Mishnayot* 1:507) maintains that he was the last of Hillel's disciples, but this is obviously forced.

> For the possible significance of the eighty figure, see *Or ha-Chaim* to Exodus 1:5.

26. *Me'iri,* R. Samuel Strashun (*Rashash*) and *Tiferet Israel* maintain that Hillel and Menahem agreed on the halakha; this would support our view that their outlook was extremely similar.

> However, see Maimonides (Mishnah) and Bertinoro who believe that Menahem did not rule on the question. This is difficult.

27. *Jewish Encyclopedia* 5:224 and 8:467.

28. *Jewish Law and Lore,* p. 101.

> The stance of Geiger and others that the Menahem of the Mishnah was Menahem son of Judah—who was a patriot leader against the Romans, and is considered by some to have been a Teacher of Righteousness of the Essenes—is difficult, to say the

least. If he had served with Hillel about 30 or 20 B.C.E., could he have still been active at Masada during 66–70 C.E.?

29. Kohler (*Jewish Encyclopedia* 8:467) seeks to establish four diverse Talmudic views with regard to Menahem's departure from the Pharisees. L. Ginzberg creates three, but is silent on the Jerusalem Talmud's second version. Our stance shall remain that the Babylonian and Jerusalem Talmuds represent the same two positions.

(L. Ginzberg's position [*On Jewish Law,* p. 251] that the Nasi Jose ben Joezer was known to all as an Essene seems open to question. The Mishnah's identification of him as Hasid of the Priesthood was set to writing hundreds of years later! It is possible, however, that the *Kohanim* among the Essenes—whose primary purpose for joining would have been to maintain a high state of levitical purity—did so openly.

With regard to Menahem, Ginzberg cannot believe that he served as Av Bet Din while known as an Essene; but isn't it entirely possible that Herod caused his identity to become known? Herod was fond of him for having foretold his rise to power, and surely made no secret of it.

As for Ginzberg's assumption that the Essenes were further removed from the Pharisees in Menahem's time than in the days of Jose ben Joezer, we can only ask: What is his source?)

30. Josephus mentions nothing, nor does the Talmud. Could the second most important rabbinic authority of the time, along with one hundred and sixty elite disciples, simply vanish?

31. Pp. 178 and 188 in Feldheim edition.

32. End Ch. 18; p. 218, Feldheim edition. Luzzatto stresses the complexity of Hasidism, and Chapter 19—describing it—is the longest of the work. His most oft-repeated description seems to be that the Hasid seeks to give pleasure (*Nahat Ruah*) to his Creator.

33. The Amora is mentioned thrice in Chapter 19. His name was actually Abba (see Note 19), and the initial denotes Rabbi.

34. Cf. statement of Resh Lakish (Shabbat 63A) advising one not to live in the neighborhood of an unlearned Hasid.

35. P. 269, Feldheim edition.
36. "All the corpses . . . killed through Gedaliah . . ." (Jeremiah 41) is interpreted by the Talmud as if he were the murderer (Niddah 61A). There is no question, however, that he was personally considered a righteous man (Rosh Ha-Shanah 18B), as his murder is still commemorated annually by a fast on the day following Rosh Ha-Shanah.
37. Bar Kamtza, a Jew who harbored a personal grudge against the Pharisees, caused a blemish in a sacrifice sent by the Roman Emperor. The Rabbis—according to the law—were prepared to accept it, but R. Zechariah objected.
38. The mere fact that Shammai's arrival caused the creation of two major and opposing Schools of Pharisees, Bet Shammai and Bet Hillel—a situation that seldom existed in earlier times or afterward—is ample evidence of the strife and division it caused in Jewish life. Although the Rabbis referred to both schools' rulings as "the words of the Living God" (Jerusalem Talmud, Berakhot 1:7), the Talmud compares the day Bet Shammai gained complete ascendancy and passed eighteen measures, overruling Bet Hillel, to the day the Golden Calf was built (Shabbat 17A). From about 70 C.E. onward, the opinion of Bet Hillel was universally accepted as the correct halakha.

    Cf. our second chapter, "Hillel's Convert," where we demonstrated that Shammai and Hillel also disagreed on whether Gentiles could achieve salvation outside Judaism through observance of the Noahide Commandments, with Hillel maintaining the affirmative view.
39. Cf. Damascus Document, where the Pharisees criticized are accused of encroachment (*Masigei Gvul*).
40. Eisenstein's interpretation of the Talmud (Shabbat 121B) as a criticism of the Essenes (*Otzar Israel,* Hasidim) is not valid, as Raba Bar R. Huna is simply stating that he disagreed with their ruling concerning killing harmful snakes or scorpions on the Sabbath (see Rashi). Indeed, the Talmud quotes R. Huna, Raba's father, as agreeing with the Essenes.

    As for the position of Eisenstein and Kohler (*Jewish Encyclopedia* 5:231) that the Mishnah's criticism (Sotah 20A) of the

Hasid fool (e.g., one who would hesitate to save a drowning woman) applied to the Essenes—one can only express surprise! Would they suppose that the same Mishnah's disapproval of the Pharisee hypocrite should be extended to all Pharisees?

Some scholars have made much of the fact that the sect might have used a different calendar than that of normative Judaism. But the evidence involved is so contradictory and inconclusive that the issue does not lend itself to logical discussion.

It would appear then that the only serious criticism of the Essenes to be found in the Talmud is that of Abbaye, and that is related to the part they played in the founding of Christianity.

41. *Karban ha-Edah*'s identification of their mission as a reconciliation with the Gentiles would be in line with our position in Chapter Two (Hillel's Convert Revisited) which maintains that the Essenes hoped Christianity would aid the Jews in their imminent exile as well as bring salvation to the Gentiles. According to the commentary of *Pnei Moshe*, the last part of the text would refer to the fact that Christians later turned against Judaism.

42. See Chapter 6 where on the basis of further Talmudic research we shall establish that it was Bet Shammai's practice to take their nieces as second wives. In the event of the husband's death, this would have led to a case involving levirate marriage (*yibum*) in which Bet Hillel considered Bet Shammai's children to be bastards. This would be the ultimate explanation for the strong condemnation of the Pharisees contained in the Damascus Document.

ADDENDA

pp. 55–56. Jesus' most well-known parable is surely that of the Good Samaritan who came to the aid of a beaten man, after a Jewish priest and levite had passed him by (Luke 10). His view of the Samaritans seems to compare with that of R. Simeon ben Gamaliel (Hullin 4a)—a great-grandson of Hillel—who held that the Samaritans were more observant of the commandments they had adopted than the Jews themselves. R. Eliezer of Bet Shammai held (ibid.) that the Samaritans could not be trusted in the observance of the commandments.

page 67, note 32. See Jesus' statement (John 8:29) "I always do those things that please Him."

4.

THE ARREST OF RABBI ELIEZER AND ITS RELATIONSHIP TO THE BELIEFS OF THE MINIM (JEWISH-CHRISTIANS)

One of the most bizarre incidents to have ever befallen a sage of the Mishnah is the arrest (or kidnaping) of Rabbi Eliezer ben Hyrcanus (Avodah Zarah 16B, Tosefta Hullin 2:6, Midrash Kohelet Rabbah 8:1).[1] It appears to have occurred during the height of the controversy with the Minim (Jewish-Christians), sometime around the turn of the first and second centuries C.E. A divergence in the textual opening between the Babylonian Talmud and the earlier Tosefta has led to two versions of the incident: the Tosefta clearly indicates an arrest by the Romans on suspicion that the sage adhered to the troublesome Jewish-Christian sect's doctrine, while the Talmud might well be interpreted as a kidnaping by the Minim in an effort to forcefully convert R. Eliezer to their views. Rashi (*ad loc.*) and Maimonides (*Igeret Hashmad*) have adopted the latter stance, while contemporary historians[2] have unanimously accepted the earlier Tosefta's version. The historians' reluctance to accept the interpretations of Rashi and Maimonides appears to be predicated not only on the earlier character of the Tosefta, but also because the Talmud could be understood similarly, and because of the vast documentation currently available pertaining to Roman persecution of Jewish-Christians.

It might be mentioned here that there is an unfortunate paucity of material on this incident in traditional Talmudic commentaries. But no matter whether kidnaping or arrest, the event is best understood by assuming that those who took him prisoner believed that he secretly harbored the beliefs of the sectarians. If it was the Romans, they would have wanted to prosecute him; if it was the Minim, they wished him to confess his view openly.[3] It should also be pointed out that the term "Minim" in Talmudic literature could also refer to other heretics or sectarians aside from Jewish-Christians. But scholars generally agree that the reference here is to Jewish-Christians because the incident occurred during the latter part of the first century, and also because there is a reference in the Talmudic text—as will be noted later—to Jacob of Kefar-Sekaniah, a well-known Jewish-Christian.

Before continuing with the subsequent turn of events, it would be only proper to reacquaint ourselves with the important standing of R. Eliezer (or Rabbi Eliezer the Great, as he was called) amongst the sages of the Mishnah. He was originally one of the outstanding disciples of R. Johanan ben Zakkai, the leading sage at the time of the Second Temple's destruction in 70 C.E. He and another disciple, R. Joshua ben Hananiah, carried R. Johanan out surreptitiously from Jerusalem in a coffin in order to negotiate the future of the Jews with Vespasian (Gittin 56B). After the death of R. Johanan, R. Eliezer and R. Joshua were recognized as the most prominent leaders of rabbinic Judaism. R. Johanan once remarked (Avot 2:8) that if all Jewish scholars were in one scale of a balance and R. Eliezer in the other, he would outweigh them all. He also compared him to a "cemented cistern that loses not a drop."

R. Eliezer later became the brother-in-law of Rabban Gamaliel of Yavneh, President of the Sanhedrin, and was a

teacher of many disciples, including Rabbi Akiva. He was the
author of Pirkei D'Rabbi Eliezer, a Midrashic work, purportedly the first rabbinic book to appear following the close of
the Bible.

It should not be omitted here that he was eventually excommunicated by the sages for refusing to accept the authority of the majority opinion (Bava Mezia 59B). He insisted that
he had never stated aught that he had not received from his
teachers, and would not forsake their view, the majority notwithstanding. Later writers have expressed the opinion that
the ban did not proscribe him from teaching.[4] Since his students will soon enter the channel of events following his arrest, we might then note that it makes no difference whether
the incident took place before or after the excommunication.

The brief biographical facts can only serve to magnify
the mystery to its proper dimensions. How could such a leading Tanna—not only in his own time, but of the entire Mishnaic period—have been suspected of harboring the beliefs of
the Jewish-Christian sectarians?

Returning now to the text, R. Eliezer was brought before
a judge. When asked how an elder such as he could be interested in such matters, he replied that he accepts the judge's
decision. The latter thought that R. Eliezer meant him,
whereas the sage had in mind his Father in Heaven. The
judge's vanity caused him to free the rabbi.

Following his release, R. Eliezer was greatly troubled
over the arrest. His disciples tried to comfort him, but without
success. R. Akiva then suggested that perhaps the sage had
had some contact with the Minim and been pleased by it. R.
Eliezer recalled that he had once met Jacob of Kefar-Sekaniah,[5] a Min, who related to him a halakha in the name of Jesus,
and it had pleased him.

This, in brief, concludes the textual account, and I have chosen not to delve here into the minor variations to be found in the three sources—that of Tosefta, Talmud and Midrash. The reader who wishes to pursue this can do so on his own. But as mentioned earlier, the prime goal of this chapter is an analysis of the events, and then to propose a practical cause for the suspicion in the first place.

A careful reading of the text suggests that neither R. Akiva nor R. Eliezer was trying to find a cause for the suspicion of R. Eliezer, but only a reason as to why he deserved such punishment from Heaven. This seems implied in R. Samuel Edel's brief comment (*Maharsha*), by stressing R. Eliezer's statements, "I said not a word to him," and "I thereby transgressed what is written in the Torah. . . ." *Maharsha* points out that R. Eliezer should have turned away from the heretic as soon as he approached and made his initial remark, rather than remain and listen to the halakha. His few words are the only ones I could find among the traditional commentaries.

Turning to secular scholars, Robert Travers Herford[6] quotes Heinrich Graetz as interpreting the meeting with Jacob the Min as the cause for the suspicion. Graetz assumes that R. Eliezer had intercourse with Jewish-Christians, and the meeting with Jacob took place shortly before the arrest. Herford correctly exposes Graetz's error by pointing out that R. Eliezer did not even recall the event until reminded of it by R. Akiva's remark. Judah Eisenstein[7] also attributes the arrest to Minim reporting R. Eliezer's association with them to the Romans, but Herford's criticism applies to him as well. Aside from this, Graetz and Eisenstein stand corrected by R. Eliezer's remark, "I spoke not a word to him." The rabbi thus shows that he was taken aback by the heretic's approach.

Herford favors an interval of some years between the meeting with Jacob and the arrest, and considers the latter event to have taken place about 109 C.E., during the perse-cution of Christians under Trajan. He supposes R. Eliezer to have been about seventy at the time. Professor Joseph Klausner[8] quotes Hirsch P. Chajes as giving the year of the ar-rest to be 95 C.E., the time of Domitian's persecution, and as-sumes that the sage was then about sixty years of age. Klausner considers it easily possible that he encountered Ja-cob, the Jewish-Christian, some twenty-five or thirty years earlier, about the year 60 C.E.

All this, of course, does not clarify the original puzzle as to why the sage was suspected. It becomes evident then that the answer must be found in some known teaching of R. Eli-ezer given in the Talmud. Since hundreds of them are to be found, one realizes the difficult task at hand.

Herford, the Christian scholar, gives up at this point, by surmising, "It is possible that some popular opinion con-nected him with the Christians." Professor Klausner—who is said to have gathered material for decades while preparing to write his *Jesus of Nazareth*—explores two such possibilities:[9] R. Eliezer's statement (Sotah 48B), "He who has bread in his bas-ket and says 'What shall I eat tomorrow?' belongs to them who are little in faith," and his short prayer, "Do Thy will in heaven above . . ." (Berakhot 29B), both of which bear some resemblance to passages in the Gospels.[10] One must express reservations toward Professor Klausner's thesis, as many Jew-ish ideas are to be found in the Christian Bible. An examina-tion of any Tanna quoted extensively in the Mishnah would probably reveal some similarity somewhere to sayings of the Gospels, yet none of them was ever suspected of harboring Jewish-Christian beliefs. It becomes evident, then, that we must find the sage to have expressed some statement going to the very core of the Jewish-Christians' creed, or possibly a statement that caused their heretical stance in the first place.

(I should stress at this point that the search for scholarly truth can lead one to strange crossroads which he did not intend traversing when starting his journey.)

It becomes necessary at this point to briefly review once again Judaism's outlook on religion amongst the Gentiles. According to the Talmud (Sanhedrin 56A–59B), the basic seven Noahide Commandments have been binding on the human race since the time of Adam. However, the Talmud (Sanhedrin 105A) and Tosefta (Sanhedrin Ch. 13) record a dispute between R. Eliezer and R. Joshua over whether a Gentile who observes the Noahide commandments merits a share in the World to Come. All agree that these universal rules are incumbent upon the entire human race, but R. Eliezer and R. Joshua disagreed as to whether a Gentile's observance of them entitled him to salvation in the afterlife. R. Eliezer of Bet Shammai adopted the view that no salvation is possible outside of Judaism and its 613 commandments; R. Joshua of Bet Hillel holds that the Gentile who observes the Noahide Laws does merit a share in the World to Come.[11] The halakhists have accepted R. Joshua's view (Maimonides, *Melakhim* 8:11, *et al.*), and such Gentiles are usually referred to as the Hasidim (righteous ones) of the Nations.

It is well known that the early Jewish-Christians in Jerusalem (the Minim) carried on a dispute with Paul (Paul of Tarsus), known as the Apostle to the Gentiles, over whether to admit Gentiles to the Mother Church (Acts 15). The Jewish-Christians were opposed to the admittance of non-Jews, and based their stance on the opinion of certain Pharisees who said "It is necessary to circumcise them, and to command them to keep the law of Moses" (Acts 15:5). Paul fought for the admittance of the uncircumcised. Since both parties to the dispute came from Orthodox Jewish backgrounds, it would appear that some disagreement on Jewish tradition must have existed between them. What could it have been?

Rabbi Jacob Emden has expressed the view that the original intent of Jesus and Paul was to bring knowledge of the Noahide Commandments to the Gentiles, while the Jews should continue their adherence to Judaism (*Sefer Shimmush* and appendix to *Seder Olam*).[12] We have also mentioned earlier that evidence exists in Jewish sources (Talmud, Sanhedrin 57A and Maimonides, *Melakhim*, Ch. 8) indicating that Moses obligated the Jews to bring knowledge of the Noahide Commandments to the Gentiles.[13] It should also be added that R. Emden's stance has been rejected by most scholars, and his letter outlining it has received scant attention.

I would wonder, though, whether R. Emden's thesis might not throw light on the dispute of Paul with the Jewish-Christians. Jesus of Nazareth had spoken of his Church as a vehicle of salvation, but had probably never made himself too clear during the year or so of his ministry. The question then arose after his death as to whether Gentiles could indeed achieve salvation outside of Judaism. Since the dispute between Paul and the Minim took place during the times of R. Eliezer and R. Joshua, I believe it ran along the same principles as the dispute between the two sages recorded in the Talmud. The Minim adopted R. Eliezer's view that no salvation was possible for Gentiles even if they observed the Noahide Commandments, and therefore assumed that Jesus must have intended to be a savior of practicing Jews only. R. Emden refers to Paul as "a scholar, an attendant of Rabban Gamaliel the Elder," and of course Paul would have known that the correct halakha was that of R. Joshua of Bet Hillel (R. Gamaliel had been a grandson of Hillel). He understood that the thrust of Jesus' mission was the salvation of the Gentiles, through a religion based upon the Noahide Commandments.

It was the Minim's adoption of R. Eliezer's Shammaite view that led them to heresy, and also to misrepresent the mission of Jesus and to distort his teachings.

With the help of Rabbi Emden's thesis,[14] there appears to be no further mystery as to why R. Eliezer ben Hyrcanus was arrested or kidnaped on the suspicion of being a Jewish-Christian.

(This Talmudic text and others also indicate that the term "Minim" employed by the Talmud to describe Jewish-Christians applied to those who endeavored to incorporate Christological teachings into Judaism and also to convince other Jews to adopt their views—unlike Paul, who taught that each should adhere to the faith in which he was called [1 Corinthians 7], as pointed out by Rabbi Emden in his letter.)

Having solved our original question through the aid of R. Jacob Emden's positive writings concerning Jesus and Paul, I must confess to the initial puzzlement I experienced when contrasting them with his unrelenting attacks on his great rabbinic contemporary, R. Jonathan Eybeschuetz. It would be safe to say that in all Jewish history, no Torah sage ever accused another of the sins R. Jacob attributed to R. Jonathan. He not only asserted that the latter was a covert adherent of the false messiah, Shabbetai Zevi, but also that he participated in their kabbalistic blasphemies, secret sexual activities, etc.

I finally solved the puzzle for myself by asking another question. How do we explain the fact that Paul of Tarsus does not appear to have ever been even remotely criticized by the rabbis of the Talmud? Having at one time been an attendant of Rabban Gamaliel the Elder, didn't he deserve to be branded as some type of traitor to rabbinic Judaism?

The answer appears to be found in what the great rabbis

of Israel have always considered to be their prime function—
that of preserving the pure teachings of Judaism amongst its
faithful adherents. When members of their community posed
as Orthodox Jews, but also adopted strange new beliefs which
were not recognized as belonging to the ancient tradition—
and this was true of both the Jewish-Christians and the Shabbateans—then these rabbis rose as lions to defend the pure
traditions of the faith. In ancient times, the Tosefta (Hullin
2:6) records the breakoff of all relations with the Jewish-
Christians, and a special prayer was even introduced against
them in the Amidah (Berakhot 28B). Because of the Minim,
Jesus may have also suffered criticism from later rabbis. (I say
"may," because nothing explicitly referring to him seems to
be contained in the Talmud.) A similar ban was invoked by
the eighteenth century rabbis against the Shabbateans, and,
interestingly, R. Emden included a phrase against them into
his prayer book.[15]

Since there was some suspicion against R. Jonathan, R.
Emden would not spare even him. Now that the dust has settled, one can find the two rabbis' books alongside one another
in the finest Jewish homes.

However, Paul of Tarsus didn't bother the Jews, and instead devoted all his energies to bringing Christian teachings
to the Gentiles. It would appear to me that the rabbis were
only too happy to see those outside Judaism learn of God and
the Bible. Paul said, "Everyone should remain in the state in
which he was called" (1 Corinthians 7:17–20).

In the last analysis, Judaism's attitude toward those who
have come under a cloud of suspicion has been summed up
by R. Joshua ben Perachiah, whom some consider to have
been the teacher of Jesus of Nazareth.[16] This sage taught
(Avot 1:6), "Judge all men in the scale of merit."

NOTES

1. Also Yalkut Shimoni, Micah 1 and Proverbs 5.
2. *Encyclopedia Judaica* 6:622; *Jewish Encyclopedia* 5:114; *Otzar Israel* 2:29; Wilhelm Bacher, *Aggadot Tannaim* 1:81; Joseph Klausner, *Jesus of Nazareth,* p. 37; Robert Travers Herford, *Christianity in Talmud and Midrash,* p. 140, *et al.*
3. While Rashi identifies the kidnapers as Jewish-Christians, Maimonides in *Igeret Hashmad* describes them as heretics who denied supernatural religion and prophecy. Cf. *Yad, Hilkhot Teshuvah* 3:7, where he enumerates five types of Minim. But even Maimonides is best understood if these Minim suspected him of a dual loyalty to Jewish-Christian beliefs, and hence that he was insincere in his religious convictions.
4. R. David Luria, in his introduction to Pirkei D'Rabbi Eliezer, concludes that it was not a full ban, but limited to entering within his four cubits. This was intended to cause it to be embarrassing for him to come to the House of Study or for his students to learn with him. But he was not actually proscribed from studying with them. Aaron Hyman, *Toledot Tanna'im,* takes the view that the ban applied only to his rabbinic colleagues, and not at all to his students.
5. The Tosafists identify him as Jacob the Min who was a faith-healer (Avodah Zarah 27B). The editor of the Soncino Talmud believes him to have been either James the son of Alphaeus (Mark 3) or James the Little (*ibid.* 15).
6. *Christianity in Talmud and Midrash,* p. 144.
7. *Otzar Israel* 2:29.
8. *Jesus of Nazareth,* p. 40.
9. *Ibid.,* p. 44.
10. Klausner believes that the first can be likened to Matthew 6:30–34, while the second resembles the prayer taught by Jesus to his disciples, Matthew 6:9–11, and Luke 11:2.
11. In Chapter Two, "Hillel's Convert Revisited," I have sought to identify this dispute as the continuation of a similar earlier one between Hillel and Shammai (Shabbat 31A).

It might be remembered that both R. Eliezer and R. Joshua studied under R. Johanan ben Zakkai, who received the Tradition from Hillel and Shammai. His two leading students evidently split along these lines, with R. Eliezer being identified as a member of the school of Shammai, and R. Joshua adhering to Bet Hillel. R. Eliezer and R. Joshua are on record as opposing each other along the lines of the two schools (see Tosefta Arakhin 4:3 and Tosefta Shabbat 1:8, as well as Shabbat 153B).

12. In his commentary *Lechem Shamayim* to Avot 4:11, R. Emden traces the survival and strength of Christianity and Islam to the Mishnah's teaching, "Every assembly that is for the sake of Heaven will in the end be established." He notes that both these faiths have accepted the seven Noahide Commandments.

13. In earlier chapters, I discussed the recent evidence from the Dead Sea Scrolls linking Christianity with the Essenes.

14. R. Emden's thesis helps solve other ancient mysteries as well. For example, scholars have uprooted mountains to understand why Christianity's founder called the Pharisees (*perushim*) hypocrites (Matthew 23)—especially since he himself said that they sit upon the seat of Moses (*ibid.*).

However, in light of R. Eliezer's view that Gentiles who observe the Noahide Commandments do not merit a share in the World to Come, and our position that Shammai shared R. Eliezer's stance (see note 11, and Chapter Two, "Hillel's Convert Revisited"), we may be fairly certain that Jesus was referring to Shammai and his school. It must be realized that the Pharisees during the first century C.E. were dominated by the schools of Shammai and Hillel. (Shammai died 30 C.E., about the same time Jesus was crucified; Hillel died about 10 C.E., and this might have caused some weakening of his school's influence.) Since Shammai was reluctant to accept converts to Judaism (Shabbat 31A), and he also denied salvation to Gentiles even if they observed the Noahide Commandments, one can attempt to rationalize Jesus' charge of hypocrisy. It would certainly be difficult to square Shammai's view with the Torah's emphasis on fairness and just reward to all men. (It should be recalled that the Talmud itself recommended that one adopt Hillel's attitude toward the converts, and not Shammai's. Shabbat 30B, bottom line; cf. Avot D'Rabbi Nathan, Ch. 15.)

According to this interpretation, we would have to assume that Shammai and his school constituted the majority of the Pharisees at the time Jesus made his remark. The popular perception that the halakha is always decided in accordance with Bet Hillel is only true from the time the *Bat Kol* (Heavenly Voice) was heard in Yavneh declaring the halakha in their favor (70 C.E. or later. Jerusalem Talmud, Berakhot 1:7). It seems quite clear from the discussion of the Talmud (Yevamot 14A) that during the century prior to that the majority status shifted from one school to the other. In one case, the Mishnah (Shabbat 13B) tells of an instance when the school of Shammai gained ascendancy and passed eighteen rules in one day. The editor of the Soncino Talmud cites several opinions as to when this took place, but Zacharias Frankel's view placing it at the beginning of the division of the two schools seems correct, as the Talmud states that Hillel was present at the time (*ibid.*, 17A).

It would seem in general that the Founder of Christianity's well-known criticism of the Pharisees (Matthew 23) is directed specifically against the school of Shammai—who evidently constituted a majority at the time—and not the school of Hillel.

He begins by bidding his listeners to do all the Pharisees command, since they have taken Moses' seat. Jesus shows his allegiance here to rabbinic Judaism.

Then he brands them as hypocrites and accuses them of placing heavy loads on men's shoulders. This appears to be an obvious reference to Bet Shammai, who almost always adopted the more stringent view and passed difficult measures.

He then accuses the Pharisees of liking to be called Rabbi, and reminds his listeners that he that shall humble himself shall be exalted. This might well be a reference to the fact that the humble members of Bet Hillel always quoted the opinion of Bet Shammai before their own in the House of Study (Eruvin 13B).

His next scathing remark appears in line with the early part of this footnote: "For you lock the doors of the Kingdom of Heaven in men's faces . . . for you compass sea and land to make one proselyte. . . ." The latter quote would refer to Shammai's reluctance to accept converts to Judaism, while by "locking the doors" he meant Bet Shammai's view denying salvation even to those Gentiles who observed the Noahide Commandments. This leads into his charge of letting the weightier matters of the Law go—justice, mercy . . . It has been pointed out by the kabbalists that the school of Hillel represented mercy (*Hesed*).

We might recall here the Talmud's statement (Shabbat 17A) that the day Bet Shammai gained complete control and passed the eighteen measures was as troublesome for Israel as the day the Golden Calf was built.

15. It would appear that his reference to Minim in the paragraph prior to the *Havdalah* service for Saturday night seems to be directed at the Minim of his time, the Shabbateans.

16. Abraham ibn Daud (1110–1180) writes in his *Sefer Hakabbalah* (Jewish Publication Society Edition, p. 15), "Jewish historians claim that Joshua ben Perachiah was the teacher of Yeshua Hanotzri" (Jesus of Nazareth).

Ibn Daud also cites a tradition which places Jesus during the reign of Alexander Yannai, or several decades earlier than the Jesus of the Gospels. Nahmanides also refers to such a tradition (*Vikuakh Ha-Ramban*, Mossad edition, p. 306), as does R. Jacob Tam (Tosafists, Shabbat 104B, but censored in contemporary texts). This has given rise to speculation that another Yeshua Hanotzri existed, and the two have been confused with one another.

R. Jehiel Heilprin (*Seder ha-Dorot*, p. 151) cites Talmudic evidence to demonstrate that two men known as Yeshua Hanotzri lived during the times of the Mishnah.

5

HASIDIM OF THE NATIONS: PARALLEL DEFINITIONS

During the first century C.E., a dispute arose among the sages[1] of Israel as to whether Gentiles could find salvation outside Judaism. The halakha is accepted in favor of the affirmative view, and since the Noahide Commandments are the only system of laws known to Jewish tradition as binding upon all humanity, their observance is understood as the vehicle of salvation. The seven basic Noahide Commandments consist of the prohibitions against idolatry, blasphemy, killing, stealing, sexual sins, the eating of a limb from a living animal (cruelty to animals), and the obligation to establish courts of justice.[2]

Rabbi Jacob Emden has expressed the view that the original intent of Jesus and Paul was to bring knowledge of the Noahide Commandments to the Gentiles, while the Jews should continue their adherence to Judaism (*Sefer Shimmush* and Appendix to *Seder Olam*). In earlier chapters, I have attempted to demonstrate that the many similarities of language and practice noted between the Christian Bible and the earlier Dead Sea Scrolls of the Essenes can be best understood by assuming that the Essene hasidim sought to spread knowledge of the Noahide Commandments to the Gentiles. We noted that the Talmud (Sanhedrin 57A) and Maimonides (*Melakhim,* Ch. 8) indicate that Moses obligated the Jews to spread knowledge of the Noahide Commandments to all mankind.[3] Studies of the Scrolls leave little doubt that Jesus and Paul were well acquainted with the writings of the Essenes.

The earliest rabbinic sources refer to those Gentiles who merit a share in the World to Come as the *Zaddikim* (righteous ones) of the Nations,[4] although Moses Maimonides, the most important post-Talmudic legal authority—along with others—employs the term *Hasidim* (pious ones) of the Nations.[5] The term "*Hasid*" is usually understood as denoting a more advanced level of religious attainment than "*Zaddik*."[6] But no matter which, both *Hasid* and *Zaddik* are recognized in Jewish literature as involving action above and beyond the letter of the Law.[7] It follows, then, that the salvation of the Gentiles—according to Jewish tradition—can only be secured by observance of the Noahide Commandments beyond the actual demands of the Torah.[8] Talmudic sources, however, are not explicit with regard to what mode of action this might consist of, and a definition of the halakha is warranted.

Maimonides states (*Melakhim* 8:11) that the Hasidim of the Nations who merit a share in the World to Come are those who accept the Noahide rules because God commanded them in the Torah, and informed us through Moses that they are obligatory upon Gentiles; but if one observes them as a result of his own reasoning, he is not considered of the Hasidim of the Nations.[9] It is manifest, then, from Maimonides that the salvation of the Gentiles as Hasid or Zaddik is dependent on acceptance of the Noahide Commandments as divinely ordained by the Torah of Moses. This belief in the Torah of Moses is not rooted in the Noahide Commandments themselves, but is an act of Hasidism, above and beyond the letter of the Law.

It is therefore worthy of note that the only statement of Jesus of Nazareth to be found in the Talmud is "I come not to destroy the Law of Moses nor to add to the Law of Moses" (Shabbat 116B).[10] This quotation is introduced to the text in order to ascertain Jesus' view of the binding character of the Torah for all time,[11] and is identifiable with his exhortation in the Sermon on the Mount (Matthew 5:17), "Do not suppose that I have come to abolish the Torah. I did not come to abolish, but to fulfill. I tell you this: So long as heaven and earth endure, not a letter, not a stroke, will disappear from the Torah until it is achieved. If any man therefore sets aside even the least of the Torah's demands, and teaches others to do the same, he will have the lowest place in the Kingdom of Heaven, whereas anyone who keeps the Torah, and teaches others so, will stand high in the Kingdom of Heaven."[12] These words—which he surely considered as central to his message of salvation—are followed almost immediately by "For I say unto you, that except your righteousness shall exceed the righteousness of the Scribes and Pharisees, ye shall in no case enter into the Kingdom of Heaven."

I believe that this latter statement—which some have misconstrued as a criticism of the Rabbis—is actually his concept of the halakha concerning the Hasidim of the Nations, and seems to correspond exactly with Maimonides' view. He surely realized that many would misunderstand and corrupt his teachings in future times. He therefore explained to his followers that whereas the 613 commandments of the Torah enjoined upon the Jews (the Scribes and Pharisees) ensure them a share in the afterlife without going beyond the letter of the Law, the salvation of the Gentiles demands an act of Hasidism[13]—and that is to observe the Noahide Commandments because they are contained in the Law of Moses.

I have noticed that many Christians are currently exploring relationships with other Gentile faiths. In this respect it might be worthy to note that R. Meir Simhah Ha-Kohen of Dvinsk, in his classic twentieth century work on Maimonides

(*Or Same'ah, Issurei Biah* 14:7), believed that Maimonides did not mean to exclude from salvation all Gentiles who do not observe the Noahide Commandments because they were ordained in the Torah of Moses, but only that those who do so will receive greater reward. According to this view, by basing Christianity on the Torah of Moses, Jesus would have wished to offer his adherents the highest form of salvation. R. Meir Simhah bases his stance on a Talmudic passage (Bava Kamma 38A).

This avenue of approach—based on R. Emden's historic letter—throws new light on other frequently misunderstood words of the founder of Christianity, which have served to bring strife, rather than joy, to men of good will. For example, his statement, "No one comes to the Father but through me" (John 14), was surely addressed to Gentiles, to whom his message of salvation through the Noahide Laws was intended— and not to his fellow Jews. This was clearly his intent, since the chapter begins with his declaration, "In my Father's house there are many mansions."

We have demonstrated in earlier chapters that Yeshua haNotzri (Jesus of Nazareth) was actually a follower of the School of Hillel and the Essene Hasidim. We also explained that any criticism of the Pharisees attributed to him was in reality directed against the opposing School of Shammai, who were in control of the Pharisees at the time. By attempting to bring salvation to the non-Jewish world, he would have been following the teaching of Hillel (Avot 1:12): "Be thou of the disciples of Aaron the Priest; one who loves peace, pursues peace, loves mankind, and brings them nigh to the Torah." Hillel's admonition to love mankind and bring them nigh to the Torah is portrayed clearly in Avot D'Rabbi Nathan 12:7– 8 as pertaining to one's conduct and attitude toward Gentiles. Cf. our earlier chapter, "Hillel's Convert Revisited."

The Hebrew term *"briyot"* employed by the sage also suggests all members of humanity.

Identifying the Noahide Commandments

See the statement of Ulla (Hullin 92A) giving thirty as the number of Noahide Commandments. This third century C.E. Talmudic sage lists only three new rules in addition to the original seven, consisting of the prohibitions against homosexuality and cannibalism, as well as the imperative to honor the Torah. Rashi tersely remarks that he does not know the other Commandments referred to, a statement rare to him.

One later work, *Asarah Ma'amarot* of R. Menahem Azariah of Fano (sixteenth century), does enumerate thirty Commandments, listing the latter twenty-three as extensions of the original seven. Another later commentator (*Kol Hiddushei Maharitz Chayess* I, end Ch. 10) suggests that the additional twenty-three are not related at all to the first seven, nor based on Scripture as they are, but were passed down by tradition.

(Although these authorities seem to take for granted that Ulla's thirty Commandments included the original seven, a thorough analysis of the sage's statement would seem to indicate that he was referring to thirty additional laws.)

Maimonides (*Melakhim* 10:6) lists one additional Noahide Commandment beyond the original seven, forbidding the coupling of different kinds of animals and the mixing of trees. *Radbaz* expresses surprise that Maimonides omits castration and sorcery, which are also listed in the Baraita (Sanhedrin 56B).

R. Saadiah Gaon (tenth century) added tithes and levirate marriage to the list of Noahide Commandments, while R. Nissim Gaon (eleventh century) also enumerated listening to God's voice, knowing God, and serving Him. R. Nissim ben

Reuben Gerondi (fourteenth century) added the commandment of charity.[14]

The aforementioned R. Nissim Gaon went further to say
that all religious acts which can be understood through human reasoning are obligatory upon Jew and Gentile alike.[15]

R. Samuel ben Hophni Gaon (tenth century) also composed a list of thirty Noahide Commandments based on Ulla's
Talmudic statement, but the text appears to be incomplete.
His list includes the prohibitions against suicide and false
oaths, as well as the imperatives related to prayer, sacrifices
and honoring one's parents.[16]

It would seem that much work remains to be done in order to properly identify all of the Noahide Commandments,
their divisions and subdivisions.

In the last chapter we interpreted Jesus' criticism of the
Pharisees as hypocrites (Matthew 23) to be based primarily on
the School of Shammai's halakhic ruling denying salvation to
Gentiles even if they observe the Noahide Commandments,
as per R. Eliezer (Sanhedrin 105A). R. Eliezer was a follower
of Bet Shammai, and his rulings were always in accordance
with their views (Jerusalem Talmud, Betsah 1:4; Shabbat
130B and Tosafists ad loc.).

We have also demonstrated (see Talmud and Jewish Tra-
dition on the Essenes) that the criticism of the Pharisees contained in the Dead Sea Scrolls was directed against Bet
Shammai, since the Pharisees criticized are described (in the
Damascus Document) as practicing polygamy, and the only
Talmudic sage who can be proved to have had two wives simultaneously was R. Eliezer (based on Jerusalem Talmud,
Yevamot 13:2, Avot D'Rabbi Nathan, Ch. 16, and Sanhedrin
68A). This stance is bolstered by the fact that R. Judah ha-
Nasi, a descendant of Hillel, referred to marrying two wives
simultaneously as an act of fornication (Ketubbot 62B), the

exact term used in the Damascus Document. This throws additional light on the issue of polygamy as a dispute between Bet Shammai and Bet Hillel, as well as the latter's affinity with the Essene Hasidim. (Polygamy was not formally banned in Judaism until the tenth century C.E.).

It might be added that the denunciations of Bet Shammai by the Essenes and the founder of Christianity almost pale in vehemence when compared to the sage Dosa ben Harkinas' labeling of his brother Jonathan (Yevamot 16A) as the "first-born of Satan" (*Bkhor Satan*) for having ruled in accordance with Bet Shammai—against Bet Hillel—in a serious case concerning levirate marriage. Some commentators have actually suggested emending the text (see *Maharitz Chayess* and cf. Soncino editor) of R. Dosa's condemnation, which cannot be entertained seriously.

It might also be noted here that R. Dosa described his brother as an extremely learned man, and advised a delegation of leading rabbis not to engage in dispute with him. During the century or so that Bet Shammai actively opposed Bet Hillel (about 30 B.C.E. to 70 C.E.), they are described in many sources as having constituted a majority of the Pharisees, but in this particular discussion they are pictured as a minority group—this would have taken place after the Heavenly Voice's proclamation against them—who were adamant in maintaining their traditions because they believed themselves intellectually superior to the School of Hillel (Yevamot 14A). The Talmud (*ibid.*) appears to recognize their superior scholarship, but points to Bet Hillel's humility as the reason the halakha was eventually accepted in their favor (Eruvin 13B). The Talmud (Shabbat 17A) compares the day Bet Shammai gained ascendancy and passed the eighteen measures to the time the golden calf was built, Rashi noting that Hillel was Nasi and a meek man. It would seem, then, that Bet Hillel's claim to representing the true tradition was based chiefly on their character, which represented the spirit of Hasidism passed down by such as King David, Ezra and the "Early Hasidim."

The Tosefta (Yevamot 1:3) records that Bet Hillel and Bet Shammai did not refrain from marrying women from each other's families, except that they would notify each other if a disputed law was involved. In the particular case of levirate marriage mentioned earlier, the children of Bet Shammai would have actually been considered bastards according to Bet Hillel. The Talmud (Yevamot 14B) further states that they showed love and friendship toward one another.

However, some of their disputes reveal fundamentally different perspectives. The Tosefta (end Rosh Ha-Shanah) records a bitter exchange between the two schools over the order of prayers should Rosh Ha-Shanah or a festival fall on the Sabbath, and it would be difficult to picture them as having prayed together in the same synagogue. Yet another time (Avot D'Rabbi Nathan, end Ch. 2) we find Bet Shammai maintaining that one should teach Torah to one who is wise, humble, of good family and rich, whereas Bet Hillel holds that one should teach to all. (R. Jacob Emden seems to apologize for Bet Shammai by interpreting "rich" as one who is contented with his lot, in line with Avot 4:1.)

It was therefore probably with a sense of welcome relief that the rabbinic community received the Heavenly Voice's decree that the halakha be universally adopted in favor of the School of Hillel (shortly after 70 C.E.; Jerusalem Talmud, Berakhot 1:4; Eruvin 13B). Such sages as R. Eliezer, who insisted on clinging to the traditions of the School of Shammai even afterward, were ostracized and even excommunicated, as was indeed the fate of this great sage of Israel. That his allegiance to Bet Shammai was the ultimate cause of his excommunication is implicit in the words of R. Gamaliel of Yavneh, a descendant of Hillel who, as Nasi, placed him under the ban during the latter part of the first century C.E.: "I have not acted . . . for the honor of my paternal house, but . . . that controversies may not multiply in Israel" (Bava Mezia 59B).

NOTES

1. R. Joshua and R. Eliezer are the disputants in both Talmud (Sanhedrin 105A) and Tosefta (Sanhedrin, Ch. 13). In an earlier chapter (Hillel's Convert), we presented our view that Hillel and Shammai originally debated the issue at the beginning of the Common Era.
2. Sanhedrin 56A–59B.
3. See Chapter Two, where we interpreted two passages in the Manual of Discipline accordingly. Those cited are "To do what is good and upright . . . as He has commanded through Moses" and "To love all the sons of light."
4. Tosefta Sanhedrin 13:1. The phrase appears in Scripture and many Midrashim.
5. Yad: *Melakhim* 8:11, *Teshuva* 3:5, *Edut* 11:10.
   Our present Talmudic texts lack it, but it is found in the work of R. Meir Abulafia (*Yad Ramah,* Sanhedrin 105A), a contemporary of Maimonides, and it is generally believed that the two possessed the same texts.
6. *Mesillat Yesharim,* Ch. 13 (p. 188, Feldheim edition).
7. See Mishnah of the Hasidim, Jerusalem Talmud, Terumot 8:10, and Measure of the Hasidim, Bava Mezia 52B. As for *Zaddik,* see Bava Mezia 83A (end Ch. 6) and Rashi *ad loc.*
8. I have not found much discussion of this point in halakhic sources, perhaps because it is self-evident.
9. R. Joseph Caro, in his *Kesef Mishnah,* believes this to be an original opinion of Maimonides, not rooted in Talmudic literature.
   But see *Tzi'unei Maharan* to Maimonides who quotes a Midrash to support his stance. I have not been able to find this Midrash at its source. Still others have pointed to the Midrash Mishnat R. Eliezer (p. 121, Makor edition), which corresponds

to Maimonides' view. However, since no Talmudic support can be found, it would be best to adopt *Kesef Mishnah*'s stance.

10. In older editions the quote reads, "I come not to destroy the Law of Moses but to add to the Law of Moses." This would refer to his message of Hasidism, as outlined further in the passage.

11. The quote is actually introduced within the context of an incident involving R. Gamaliel of Yavneh, his sister Imma Shalom and a Jewish-Christian, but is clearly intended to convey Jesus' belief in the immutability of the Torah.

12. Jesus' words concerning the Law in the Sermon are stressed strongly by R. Jacob Emden to support his view that Jesus actually sought to strengthen the Torah of Moses.

13. See also his statement (Matthew 7), "Whatsoever ye would that men should do unto you, even so do ye also unto them." We suggested in Chapter Two that this too represents an act of Hasidism, since the Noahide Commandments are actually understood as negative prohibitions (Sanhedrin 58B). It is probable that Matthew 5 outlined the minimum he expected from his followers, whereas Matthew 7 depicts his conception of the true Hasid of the Nations.

14. For the sources, see the *Talmudic Encyclopedia*, 1981, p. 396.

15. *Ibid.*, p. 350.

16. *Ibid.*, pp. 395–396.

6.

THE RELATIONSHIP OF RABBI ELIEZER TO THE SCHOOL OF SHAMMAI

It is widely known to students of Talmud that two opposing schools of Pharisees—Bet Shammai and Bet Hillel—existed from about 30 B.C.E. until approximately 70 C.E. The available evidence indicates that the former usually constituted a majority of the Pharisees[1] until the latter half of the first century C.E. Following the destruction of the Temple in 70 C.E., the center of Jewish scholarship and seat of the Sanhedrin was relocated to Yavneh, where Bet Hillel's authority grew progressively.[2] Finally, according to the Talmud, a Heavenly Voice (*Bat Kol*) was heard in Yavneh proclaiming the halakha in favor of Bet Hillel.[3] The two schools are on record as having opposed each other on more than three hundred and fifty occasions, and these debates serve as the principal source of Bet Shammai's positions. The later rabbis emphatically declared (Berakhot 36B): "The opinion of Bet Shammai when it conflicts with that of Bet Hillel is no Mishnah." In other words, their views are to be considered null and void.

The conclusions of this book—and this chapter as well—demand further evidence that Bet Shammai were in control of Jewish life and institutions during the first century C.E. and the final decades B.C.E. We may first point to Betsah 20A where the School of Shammai constituted a majority in the time of Bava ben Buta, who lived during Herod's reign. The enactment of the "eighteen measures" by Bet Shammai, at

93

which time they constituted an absolute majority, seems to have also taken place shortly after the establishment of the two schools (see Tosefta Shabbat 1:8 and Tosafists, Shabbat, bottom 14B). The necessity for the Heavenly Voice's intervention in favor of Bet Hillel is in itself evidence of Bet Shammai's strong position.

Talmudic evidence in fact indicates that Bet Shammai's dominance extended throughout most of the first century. See Mishnah (Sukkah 37B) where R. Akiva notes that R. Gamaliel of Yavneh and R. Joshua waved the *Lulav* (palmbranch on the festival of Sukkot) in accordance with Bet Hillel, whereas "all the people" observed Bet Shammai's practice. Since R. Johanan ben Zakkai is not mentioned, this would have taken place about 80 C.E. or later (but before the Heavenly Voice). See also Mishnah (Yadayim 4:6) where R. Johanan ben Zakkai (who served as Nasi in 70 C.E.) disassociates himself from the Pharisees; this has caused much puzzlement amongst scholars, but according to my thesis he is identifying himself as a member of the Hasidim (Bet Hillel). Cf. Talmud (Nazir 19B–20A) where it is recorded that Queen Helena, a convert to Judaism, followed the Shammaite view of R. Eliezer (c. 40 C.E.) with regard to her *Nazirite* vow (according to the interpretation of R. Judah given by Maimonides and Bertinoro). We should also point to the Mishnah (Parah 12:4) where it is related that the people practiced in accordance with Bet Shammai's view permitting one to come in contact with red heifer sin-offering water (mixed with the ashes) which had already been used for its purpose (of purification), without contracting ritual uncleanness. The Tosefta (Parah 12:6) records that R. Gamaliel the Elder, a descendant of Hillel, strongly protested this practice—as it could lead to entering the Temple grounds in a state of impurity—but he was ignored.

I have found that certain Christian scholars too have

taken note of Bet Shammai's dominant position in Jesus' time. W.D. Davies, in his *Paul and Rabbinic Judaism* (p. 9), quotes from B.H. Branscomb, *Jesus and the Law of Moses*, p. 54: "Apparently then during the lifetime of Jesus the party of Hillel was not yet in control. . . . It means that an active and rapidly growing party within the ranks of the scholars was at the time in vigorous protest against the currently accepted interpretation of the Torah." How unfortunate that such a seeker of truth was not able to delve any further into what the "vigorous protest" consisted of.

Davies himself (*ibid.*) writes, "It is clear that it was Pharisaism, and that of the Shammaite kind, that dominated first-century Judaism." But instead of pursuing the matter, he abruptly declares, "Here we shall not attempt any exhaustive survey of Judaism in the first century." It would seem that such men were on the correct trail, but simply lacked the tools they were seeking.

Davies also insists (p. 325) that the Noahide Commandments were present in the thoughts of Paul of Tarsus, as in Romans (1 and 2). He also furnishes much scholarly evidence that Paul personally observed the 613 Commandments of Judaism throughout his lifetime (pp. 69–70). There appears no question that sincere Christian scholars too have noted the validity of Rabbi Emden's conclusions.

Yet another Christian scholar who takes note of Bet Shammai's dominant position is George Foot Moore, who writes ". . . it was perhaps only after the fall of Jerusalem that the Hillelites gained the ascendancy" (*Judaism in the First Centuries of the Christian Era* 1:81).

Eugene Fisher seems to have long suspected the similarity of Jesus' views with those of Bet Hillel, as he returns to the theme several times (*Faith Without Prejudice*, pp. 39–40).

Returning now to the subject under discussion, the two leading sages during the closing decades of the first century

C.E. were Rabbi Eliezer[4] and Rabbi Joshua, the latter being recognized as a firm adherent of Bet Hillel.[5] However, R. Eliezer was referred to as *"Shammuti"* (Shabbat 130B and Niddah 7B), because, as the Jerusalem Talmud points out frequently, he was a staunch follower of the School of Shammai, and never deviated from their teachings.[6] Rashi, the most important Talmudic commentary, also notes (Shabbat 130B) the semantic relationship of "Shammuti" with *Shamta* (excommunication), thus linking the term with the Rabbis' eventual excommunication of R. Eliezer because of his refusal to accept the authority of the majority opinion (Bava Mezia 59B).

In the first portion of this chapter we shall attempt to clarify a difficult passage of the Talmud by demonstrating that R. Eliezer frequently reveals to us specific positions of Bet Shammai—amongst them unpopular positions which were criticized by the Essenes and the founder of Christianity—not known from the recorded debates of the two Schools. The second part of the chapter will seek to ascertain as Rashi's stance that R. Eliezer was excommunicated by the Rabbis because he refused to recognize the authority of Bet Hillel even after the Heavenly Voice's intervention on their behalf.

Criticism in Gospels and Dead Sea Scrolls
of Rabbinic Laws Concerning Vows and Marriage

Talmud, Shabbat 127B: "He who judges his neighbor in the scale of merit is himself judged favorably. . . ." To illustrate this teaching, the Talmud cites a case where a certain man was engaged by an individual for three years. On the eve of the Day of Atonement he asked his employer for his wages "that I may go and support my wife and children," but the employer replied that he had nothing to give him. The unfortunate employee went home emptyhanded with a sorrow-

ful heart. After the festival, the employer visited the
employee at his home, and not only paid him his wages, but
bestowed other gifts as well. After they had eaten and drunk,
the employer asked the laborer what his thoughts had been
("of what did you suspect me?") at the time he had told him
he had nothing to pay him. "I thought," he replied, "perhaps
he has sanctified all his property to Heaven." The employer
then rejoined: "By the Temple service; it was even so! I vowed
away all my property because of my son Hyrcanus, who would
not occupy himself with the Torah, but when I went to my colleagues in the South they absolved me of all my vows. And as
for you, just as you judged me favorably, so may God judge
you favorably."

The Talmud does not furnish the identities of either the
employer or the employee. However, the *She'iltot* of R. Ahai
Gaon (Exodus 40), an eighth century C.E. work, identifies the
employer as R. Eliezer and the employee as R. Akiva. The un-
avoidable question then arises as to why the Talmud so un-
characteristically omitted their names from the narrative.

Rabbi Naphtali Zevi Judah Berlin (*ha-Neziv*), in his nineteenth century commentary to the *She'iltot* (*Ha'amek She'elah*
40:2), maintains that the incident took place early in their
lives, when the two were still totally ignorant of Jewish learning. (R. Eliezer began studying in his twenties, R. Akiva at
forty.) Therefore, in deference to the two sages, the Talmud
omitted their names. However, R. Berlin's stance raises man-
ifold difficulties.[7]

I should like to suggest an alternative approach, which
would place the incident during the time R. Akiva had already begun his studies, and had become a disciple of R. Eliezer and R. Joshua.[8] Rabbinic sources record that during the
time R. Akiva studied he worked part-time to support himself
and his family (Avot D'Rabbi Nathan 6:2),[9] and also that he
took leave of them for long periods of time (Nedarim 50A)—

which fits well with our text. R. Eliezer was well-to-do, and in a position to give him such work.[10] However, this Talmudic text proves R. Eliezer to have personally practiced two rulings of Bet Shammai which were denounced strongly by the Essenes (assuming Essene authorship of the Dead Sea Scrolls) and the Founder of Christianity—namely, that it was entirely permissible to vow all of one's belongings to the Temple in Jerusalem, even though it would reduce him to total poverty, and thus prevent him from fulfilling his obligations or paying his debts to others; and also that it was not wrong (see note 12 for a clarification of Bet Shammai's view) for a Pharisee to have two wives simultaneously. Therefore, out of due consideration for R. Eliezer, his name—along with that of his most famous disciple—was omitted from the text.

Jesus Accuses the Pharisees: "For the Sake of Your Tradition, You Have Made Void the Word of God"

With regard to the Founder of Christianity, we find him chiding the Pharisees of his time (Matthew 15) "And why do you transgress the commandment of God for the sake of your tradition? For God commanded 'Honor your father and your mother,' and 'He who speaks evil of father or mother, let him surely die.' But you say, 'If any one tells his father or his mother, what you would have gained from me is given to God, he need not honor his father.' So, for the sake of your tradition, you have made void the word of God." It is clear from our Talmudic text that this was R. Eliezer's view (having vowed away all his possessions because of Hyrcanus, he clearly believed at the time that he had no further obligations toward his son, nor toward R. Akiva, who had worked for him), and we already know from the Jerusalem Talmud that R. Eliezer never differed with Bet Shammai's position. The majority opinion however, based on scripture, and as presented in the Talmud (Arakhin 28A) and more explicitly in the Tosefta, is that one should under no circumstances dedicate all his belongings to the Temple; but if he does so, it is a valid vow and the Temple has possession (see Maimonides, *Arakhin* 6:2, and *Kesef Mishnah ad loc.*). Maimonides (*Arakhin* 8:13) describes one who makes such a vow as a fool who deserves no mercy from any charitable source. Jesus does not seem to question the validity of the vow, but only the ethical question involved in permitting such a vow and throwing one's family into abject poverty without qualm, and thus eluding all further obligation toward them—and is therefore aligning himself with what later became the majority opinion. R. Eliezer himself—probably because of the suffering caused to R. Akiva and Hyrcanus—later reverted to the other extreme, and held such a vow to be null and void (Arakhin 28A).[11]

In the parallel passages in the Gospel of Mark (7:12), Jesus adds "And you no longer let him do anything for his father or his mother." This is difficult to understand, as all the vower had to do was to appear before a rabbi or three laymen, express his regret, and he could be absolved of his vow. However, since we have identified Bet Shammai as the target of Jesus' earlier criticism, we know that the Shammaites held that one could never be released from a vow made to the Temple (Nazir 9A). Thus, this son's vow could never be annulled.

Likewise, in the Dead Sea Scrolls (Damascus Document), the Essenes criticize the Pharisees who marry two wives simultaneously, as well as their nieces. It is quite clear from the Scrolls that the Essenes did not mean to say that such acts were forbidden, but only that it was improper for Pharisees (*Perushim* or Hasidim) to adopt such practices.[12] Of the two thousand Pharisees mentioned by name in the Talmuds, not one is recorded as having practiced polygamy. However, since our Talmudic text informs us that R. Eliezer's son Hyr-

canus was born to him early in life, after he was already recognized as a sage and married to Imma Shalom—sister of R.
Gamaliel of Yavneh—it thereby presents us with evidence
that he practiced polygamy. For we know that R. Eliezer, late
in life, married his niece (Avot D'Rabbi Nathan, ch. 16); yet
Hyrcanus and his mother are both mentioned in the Talmud
as being present on the day R. Eliezer died (Sanhedrin 68A)—
thus proving that he did have two wives simultaneously, one
of them his niece.[13] Since R. Eliezer never acted contrary to
the views of Bet Shammai, we may understand that the Essenes' criticism was directed at the School of Shammai, who
practiced such custom. (R. Judah ha-Nasi, a descendant of
Hillel, referred to polygamy as fornication [Ketubbot 62B],
the exact term contained in the Damascus Document.)

    I believe then that because our text (Shabbat 127B) iden-
tifies R. Eliezer as having practiced two controversial customs
of Bet Shammai—permitting polygamy and marriage to one's
niece, as well as vowing all of one's belongings to the Temple—his name, and that of his disciple R. Akiva, were omitted
from the Talmudic text.

The Excommunication of Rabbi Eliezer

    Following a dramatic debate between R. Eliezer and the
Sages concerning a case involving Levitical purity (*Taharot*)—
at which time he refused to accept the opinion of the majority—he was excommunicated (Bava Mezia 59B).[14] According
to the Talmudic narrative, he purportedly performed three
miracles to support his stance, which failed to impress the
Rabbis.[15] He then produced a Heavenly Voice (*Bat Kol*) which
agreed with his stance, but R. Joshua dismissed this by quoting from the Bible (Deuteronomy 30:12): "It is not in
heaven."[16] The latter and R. Gamaliel of Yavneh, a descendant of Hillel, appear to have led the Rabbis in pronouncing

the ban. R. Akiva then volunteered to inform R. Eliezer of the Rabbis' resolution, declaring "Lest an unsuitable person go and inform him, and thus destroy the whole world." From that day onward, R. Eliezer was no longer associated with the inner circle of leading Pharisees. Until the day he died, every decision he had ever rendered was considered to be null and void; after his death, some were accepted as correct (Niddah 7B–8B).

In the Babylonian Talmud, we find R. Eliezer referred to as *"Shammuti"* in two sources (Shabbat 130B and Niddah 7B).[17] Rashi, the leading commentator, interprets the term at the first source as related to his excommunication (*"Shamta"* is one of several Talmudic terms for excommunication),[18] and also notes that in the Jerusalem Talmud *"Shammuti"* always refers to his association with Bet Shammai—while at the second source he mentions only that *"Shammuti"* is connected to the ban. All later rabbinic sources have understood Rashi as offering two distinct and unrelated interpretations (the ban or Bet Shammai), but that he appears to lean toward the "excommunication," or first interpretation, since it is the only one he mentions at the second source.

This understanding of Rashi has led to several objections. The Tosafists (Niddah 7B) cannot believe that R. Joshua would have referred to R. Eliezer as *"Shammuti"* (*ibid.*) if the term only denoted the ban. R. Jair Hayyim Bacharach, in his seventeenth century work *Havvat Yair* (responsa 94), cannot comprehend why all R. Eliezer's prior teachings were nullified, if we adopt Rashi's first interpretation, that *"Shammuti"* is related to the ban.[19] R. Zevi Hirsch Chajes (*Maharitz Chayyes*, Niddah 7B) expresses puzzlement as to why virtually all R. Eliezer's rulings on Levitical purity were eventually rejected by the rabbis, since the Talmud (Bava Mezia 59B) only gives one case as conflicting with the majority opinion.[20] Modern scholars such as Judah Eisenstein have noted that several other sages were excommunicated, yet were never referred to as *"Shammuti."* Another modern writer, Isaac Hirsch Weiss (*Dor*), has raised a storm of protest by concluding that R. Eliezer proved himself a conceitful man by refusing to accept the majority opinion; and rebuttals of Weiss' criticism by A. Hyman (*Toledot Tanna'im*) and Halevy (see Soncino editor) seem to be based on emotionalism.

I believe that all these difficulties can be resolved by first positing an important observation in Rashi's text (Shabbat 130B). Students of Talmud know well that when Rashi offers two varying interpretations for one Talmudic passage, he invariably states "others say," "some explain," etc., between the two interpretations. This is lacking here. In other words, I believe that Rashi is giving only one interpretation, and not two. What he is telling us is that the term *"Shammuti"* bears a double connotation (excommunication and adherent of Bet Shammai), and the Talmudic sages chose the term in order to inform us that R. Eliezer was excommunicated because he refused to accept the majority opinion of Bet Hillel—even after the Heavenly Voice's decree that the halakha be universally adopted in their favor. He defiantly maintained his loyalty to Bet Shammai, Heavenly Voice notwithstanding! And virtually all of his teachings were of Shammaite origin as well.[21]

The entire Talmudic text must now be reread as a final stand by R. Eliezer, the most outstanding adherent of Bet Shammai toward the close of the first century C.E., against what he saw as the consummate triumph of Bet Hillel. The particular case of Levitical purity (*Tanur Aknai*) which caused the confrontation is only coincidental. What was actually involved here were hundreds of laws and theological views debated by the two Schools for a full century. Bet Shammai still considered themselves intellectually superior to Bet Hillel (Yevamot 14A), and thus did not recognize the latter's majority amongst the Pharisees. As for the Heavenly Voice, even R.

Joshua, the staunch representative of Bet Hillel, agreed that it lacked final authority. But Bet Shammai could not withstand the merger of both powers simultaneously; the Heavenly Voice had spoken, and so had the majority of Pharisees on earth (see note 16)—the Halakha is as Bet Hillel!

Assuming our stance, all the difficulties appear to fade away. R. Joshua declares (Niddah 7B) that even where he knew R. Eliezer to be correct—i.e., where his view was not exclusively of Shammaite origin—it was not to be practiced so during R. Eliezer's lifetime, lest the people follow the sage in his other rulings as well. Then the third century C.E. Samuel (*ibid.*) finds four decisions concerning Levitical purity where the Halakha was later adopted in R. Eliezer's favor (i.e., they were not of Shammaite origin). This also explains why even decisions rendered by R. Eliezer many years prior to the ban could not be accepted—all of these having been of exclusive Shammaite origin. Nor was R. Eliezer being conceitful by refusing to follow the majority; he was simply on the defensive, stressing Bet Shammai's great learning, not his own. (We find the same attitude in Jonathan ben Harkinas' apparently derisive remark to R. Akiva [Yevamot 16A]—R. Jonathan having also been a latter-day leader of Bet Shammai.)

The Heavenly Voice's decree thus brought an era to a close on a note of finality.[22] But this is not to say that Bet Shammai is not remembered with reverence amongst students of Talmud. The Heavenly Voice rings clear: "Both are the words of the living God, but the Halakha is as Bet Hillel." Beneath all the turmoil and debate, we are told (Yevamot 14B): "They showed love and friendship towards one another, thus putting into practice the Scriptural text (Zechariah 8:19) 'Love ye truth and peace.' "[23] It was a war of ideas, and both sides sought to advance what they thought best for their people. The Mishnah finally tells us (Avot 5:17): "Every controversy that is for God's sake shall in the end lead to a lasting result . . . such was the controversy of Hillel and Shammai."

This is well reflected in the Sages' final visit to R. Eliezer on the day of his death (Sanhedrin 68A), R. Joshua and R. Akiva amongst them. Following his passing, R. Joshua[24] arose and exclaimed: "The vow (excommunication) is annulled!" R. Akiva, during his funeral address, quoted Elisha's parting words to Elijah (2 Kings 2:12), "My father, my father, the chariot of Israel. . . ."

NOTES

1. Cf. Chapter Three where we demonstrated that virtually all of Hillel's original disciples left to join the Essenes, and were the authors—or co-authors—of certain of the Dead Sea Scrolls. I have also pointed out in Chapter Four, note 14, that Hillel died about 10 C.E. and Shammai in 30 C.E., which would help rationalize Bet Shammai's ascendancy in Jesus' time.

2. R. Johanan ben Zakkai, who was Nasi at the time, is generally recognized to have been an adherent of Bet Hillel (see Sukkah 28A). He was succeeded by R. Gamaliel of Yavneh, a descendant of Hillel.

3. Jerusalem Talmud, Berakhot 1:4; Babylonian Talmud, Eruvin 13B.

4. In his introduction to Pirkei D'Rabbi Eliezer, R. David Luria *(Radal)* stresses R. Eliezer's preeminence in both the Oral Law and the Kabbalah. He points to the fact that he was considered the greatest of R. Johanan ben Zakkai's disciples, that he is mentioned almost twice as often as R. Joshua in the Mishnah, and that he appears to have been the principal mentor of R. Akiva, the most important figure in the development of the Oral Law (Sanhedrin 86A). Luria believes that because of all these factors, R. Eliezer was known as "The Great."

5. Historians have unequivocally identified R. Joshua with the

School of Hillel. See Ze'ev Jawitz, *Toledot Israel*, 6:35; *Otzar Israel; Encyclopedia Judaica, et al.*

6. Jerusalem Talmud: Betsah 1:4; Terumot 5:2; Yevamot 13:16, et al.

   R. Eliezer and R. Joshua are in fact on record as having opposed each other along the lines of the two schools, as in Tosefta Arakhin 4:3, Tosefta Shabbat 1:8 and Shabbat 153B. Halakhic disputes between R. Eliezer and R. Joshua were usually decided by the later rabbis in favor of the latter, surely because of his affinity with Bet Hillel.

7. First, the conversation of the employer and employee doesn't ring as an exchange between two unlearned men. Second, Berlin's interpretation presupposes a coincidental relationship between R. Eliezer and R. Akiva before the latter began studying under him, for which there is no evidence in Talmudic sources. Third, according to Pirkei D'Rabbi Eliezer, R. Eliezer did not marry until after he studied. (Avot D'Rabbi Nathan presents a conflicting view by describing him as having had a wife earlier in life.) Fourth, Talmudic sources elsewhere are quite candid in relating how they began their studies late in life. Fifth, according to R. Berlin, R. Eliezer's first wife and this son Hyrcanus both died, and the sage later had another son named Hyrcanus who was present on the day he died (Sanhedrin 68A). It is highly unusual among Jews to give a child the same name as a child who had died earlier.

   (R. Berlin actually writes that R. Eliezer acted as an ignorant man *[am ha-aretz]* by dedicating all his belongings to the Temple. He was apparently unaware of Jesus' criticism [Matthew 15] of a certain group of Pharisees who maintained that there was nothing wrong with such an act. It may also be noted that Jesus [ibid.] calls the Pharisees he criticizes "hypocrites," and we have previously demonstrated in Chapter Four, note 14, that this was principally because of Bet Shammai's position that even those Gentiles who observe the Noahide Commandments do not merit a share in the World to Come, as per R. Eliezer [Sanhedrin 105A].)

8. After six years of study, R. Akiva began learning under the two

sages (Avot D'R. Nathan, ch. 6). Aaron Hyman, *Toledot Tann-a'im*, gives the year as 53 C.E.

9. Before beginning his studies and marrying the famed Rachel, R. Akiva had another wife and at least one child (Yadayim 3:5 and Avot D'R. Nathan 6:2).

10. R. Eliezer was a landowner and belonged to a wealthy family, whereas R. Joshua labored as a needlemaker.

11. R. Berlin gives three possible rulings by the unnamed "colleagues in the South" which permitted R. Eliezer to annul his vow, but this appears to be the most likely one. We find R. Eliezer reversing himself on one other occasion (Sukkah 27A).

    R. Eliezer's reference to these rabbis—probably adherents of Bet Shammai—as "my colleagues" supports our contention that he was already a sage at the time.

12. The Torah expressly permits polygamy (Deuteronomy 21:15), and it was not officially banned in Judaism until the tenth century C.E. Virtually the only biblical support the Essenes were able to muster was that all species entering Noah's ark were in groups of two. Likewise, the composers of the Damascus Document were on weak ground when comparing marriage to a niece to that with an aunt, which is forbidden.

    What evidently seemed to irk the Essenes was that the Pharisees they criticized practiced polygamy and marriage to a niece normally and regularly—and were thus not worthy of being members of the Pharisees or Hasidim, who were supposed to observe a more stringent degree of holiness. As we note here (as well as in Chapter Three), the only Talmudic sage who can be proven to have married his niece as a second wife is R. Eliezer, and we therefore interpret the Document as an attack on Bet Shammai, whose practices were always adopted by R. Eliezer. It is therefore highly probable that Bet Shammai only practiced polygamy when marrying a niece, which seems to have been regarded as a pious act leading to superior marital harmony (cf. Yevamot 62B and Maimonides, *Issurei Biah* 2:14). Since it is further recorded that R. Eliezer married his niece at his mother's request (Jerusalem Talmud, Yevamot 13:2), it might have been regarded as an act of fealty toward family.

The composers of the Damascus Document followed up their criticism with a derogatory remark about these Pharisees' children. In an earlier chapter I identified the authors of the Document as former disciples of Hillel and Menahem, and I therefore believe this remark is connected with the serious debate between Bet Shammai and Bet Hillel concerning "The Daughter's Rival" (*Tzarat ha-Bat*, Yevamot 2A–16A)—in which Bet Hillel considered the children of Bet Shammai to be bastards. This case arose when a man married two wives, one of them his niece, and then died childless. His surviving brother (father of one of his wives) was normally obligated to take the deceased brother's childless wife in levirate marriage (*Yibum*— Deuteronomy 25:5). But since he couldn't marry his own daughter, Bet Hillel ruled that the surviving brother couldn't marry the other wife either—and if he did so, a child born of such a marriage would be considered a *mamzer* (bastard). However, Bet Shammai insisted that the surviving brother must take the other wife in levirate marriage. By often practicing polygamy and marriage with their nieces, Bet Shammai must have had many such children amongst them. (Proof for my interpretation may be brought from the fact that before launching their derogatory remark, only marriage to a brother's daughter is mentioned, and not a sister's daughter—a clear reference to levirate marriage.)

The extreme feelings generated on both sides because of this dispute may be gauged by the fact that when R. Joshua was asked for his opinion on the matter (Yevamot 15B), he expressed fear to declare his support for Bet Hillel, lest he be killed (a fanatical fringe must have existed within Bet Shammai). The sage Dosa ben Harkinas called his brother Jonathan "the first-born of Satan," because he declared his support for Bet Shammai on this issue (Yevamot 16A).

13. In his introduction to Pirkei D'Rabbi Eliezer (11A), R. David Luria believes that the Hyrcanus present when R. Eliezer died was his son by his niece, and that he married her after Imma Shalom's death. This assumption seems to conflict with our Talmudic text (Shabbat 127B), which mentions a son Hyrcanus

early in R. Eliezer's life. Aside from this, he married his niece late in life (Avot D'Rabbi Nathan 16:2), and in his conversation with her beforehand (*ibid.*), the sage hints that he could not have a normal marital life with her. Also, the only mention of R. Eliezer's children in the Talmud (Nedarim 20A) gives Imma Shalom as their mother, and it would be difficult to assume Hyrcanus, the only one mentioned by name, as having been another woman's child.

As for R.N. Berlin's contention that R. Eliezer had two sons named Hyrcanus, see the end of note 7.

14. The Talmud gives no date, but it is generally assumed to have taken place about 80 C.E. or shortly thereafter.

15. Aaron Hyman (*Toledot Tanna'im*) cites a completely natural interpretation to the third alleged miracle involving the "walls of the House of Study," by representing them as the disciples. This provides a vivid picture of the uncertainty and bewilderment that must have prevailed among the younger members of the Pharisee community.

16. The Tosafists (Yevamot 14A and Bava Mezia 59B) stress that all sages agreed that a Heavenly Voice alone could not be decisive; however, the *Bat Kol* supporting Bet Hillel came at a time when they constituted the majority among the Pharisees, thus offsetting Bet Shammai's claim that their intellectual superiority (literally "sharpness") invalidated Bet Hillel's numerical majority.

17. In Shabbat 130B, Resh Lakish quotes R. Judah ha-Nasi as expressing surprise that a ruling of R. Eliezer concerning circumcision on the Sabbath was adhered to, since he was *"Shammuti."* In Niddah 7B, R. Joshua declares that R. Eliezer's view cannot be adopted during his lifetime even where he is known to have been correct, since he was *Shammuti.*

18. The most frequent terms employed are *Niddui, Herem, Shamta* and *Nezifah.*

19. Bacharach argues that even in the case of a *Zaken Mamre* (a scholar who rebels against a decision of the Sanhedrin), his previous decisions are not voided.

(Nahmanides actually asserts that had R. Eliezer similarly defied the majority during the Temple period, he would have

been adjudged a *Zaken Mamre*. See the opening of R. David Luria's introduction to Pirkei D'R. Eliezer for all Nahmanides'
writings on the subject.)
20. *Maharitz Hayess* explicitly poses his query according to both
    interpretations of Rashi. He focuses his puzzlement on Rashi
    (Pesahim 15A), where the latter states that following the ex-
    communication, R. Joshua's view is favored over R. Eliezer's in
    all matters pertaining to levitical purity. It is clear from Chajes,
    the Tosafists, and all who assume the two interpretations, that
    the Jerusalem Talmud's linkage of R. Eliezer to Bet Shammai
    was limited to no possible disagreement between the two.
21. R. Eliezer stated on several occasions (Sukkah 28A *et al.*): "I
    have never in my life said a thing which I did not hear from my
    teacher." His teacher had been R. Johanan ben Zakkai, who re-
    ceived the Tradition from both Hillel and Shammai (Avot 2:8).
    R. Eliezer thus makes clear—in a defensive, if not defiant,
    tone—that all his views were teachings passed down from
    Shammai.
22. A sensational tradition that seems to lack a source exists, stating
    that in "the future time to come" *(le-atid lavo)* the law will revert
    in favor of Bet Shammai. Several rabbis have queried me about
    this, and, amazingly, they were under the impression that this
    belief has a Talmudic base. My research has revealed no roots
    in the Talmud or its recognized commentaries.

    The *Encyclopedia Judaica* (4:741) gives the source as R.
    Moses Graf's mystical work *Va-Yakhel Moshe* (1699), and the
    commentary *Tosafote Hadashim* (beginning of Avot) also cites it
    in the name of "the rabbi from Nikolsburg" (Graf lived in Ni-
    kolsburg). But I have searched that work, and especially the last
    several pages which deal exclusively with the two Schools, and
    I have not found such a statement. I in fact believe that this "tra-
    dition" stems from a misreading of a passage in the book.

    One rabbinic scholar recently wrote an historical work and
    mentioned the tradition's source as the sixteenth century mystic
    R. Isaac Luria. When I queried this rabbi, he admitted that he
    had never seen it in writing, nor had he ever even heard of Graf
    (most people haven't). This rabbi also raised uncertainties over

which time and place might be alluded to by the term "the future time to come."

Since this tradition evidently lacks any basis in the authoritative halakhic sources, and cannot even be found in the Kabbalistic books where it is alleged to appear, it cannot be discussed in a scholarly fashion. I might add that the comment in *Tosafote Hadashim* is given by the eighteenth century Chassidic Rabbi Levi Isaac of Berdichev who notes that he heard it in the name of the rabbi from Nikolsburg.

23. R. Samuel Edels (*Maharsha*, last note to Yevamot 14B) notes that the Talmud's evident meaning here is that where peace and love exist between the opposing parties, they can both be considered "truth." His source is Hagigah 3B where the Talmud, commenting on Ecclesiastes 12:11, "Given from one shepherd," states, "One God gave them, one leader (Moses) uttered them. . . ."

24. It might be noted here that the School of Hillel seems to have been more amenable toward discussions with those who maintained opposing religious views. Thus, R. Joshua holds such talks with Romans (Sanhedrin 90B), and attended the theological debates at Be Avidan (*Toledot Tanna'im*'s interpretation of Shabbat 152A). No such records exist concerning R. Eliezer. Hillel himself conversed patiently with heathens who disagreed with him, whereas Shammai rebuffed them (Shabbat 31A).

7

THE ROOTS OF CHRISTIAN ANTI-SEMITISM:
Bet Hillel vs. Bet Shammai

Scholars have wrestled for centuries with the seemingly anti-Jewish statements that are attributed by the Christian Bible to Jesus of Nazareth. A reading of his great attack on the Pharisees (Matthew 23) virtually leaves one in a state of shock. Is this the same person who wandered off as a boy to discuss the Torah with the Doctors of the Law at the Temple (Luke 2:46)? In this latter passage he seems to exhibit a profound love for the Torah, a love which one can discern on the countenances of many Jewish youngsters to this day. What could possibly have impelled him at a later date to refer to these rabbis as hypocrites, vipers and even murderers? It is quite clear that he considered these Pharisees as being worthy of death. And for two thousand years now, Christians seem to have been able to cleanse their consciences following pogroms or a holocaust by simply reading passages such as these.[1] Nor have such statements endeared him to the people from whom he sprang.

Or take the passages (John 8 and Revelation 2 and 3) where he speaks of Jews as children of the devil, or of their synagogues as "synagogues of Satan." In the Middle Ages the Church actually thought of the Jews as being less than human because of these statements, and persecuted them as well.

The reader may ask why we should even bring up such

matters. If we simply hush up such passages, they will be forgotten and abandoned by Christians. I do not think so. They are there in the Christian Bible, and will eventually surface again.

Could it be that Jesus wasn't quoted correctly in the Gospels? Christians will certainly insist that his words were faithfully recorded and preserved. Others may suggest that he was mistaken about the Pharisees, that perhaps he didn't know them well enough! A careful reading of the attack would seem to indicate that he knew them very well, and for many years. But perhaps he didn't mean to be taken seriously, one might suggest. A careful reading will surely dismiss any such conception.

Why, then? What brought him to such a complete break with his people, with their revered scholars, what caused him to turn his back on them and scorn everything his family had held sacred for centuries? How could he bring himself to call the Jews of his time children of the devil, and their places of worship synagogues of Satan?

Or was he really anti-Jewish or anti-traditionalist at all? I have suggested earlier in this book that he possessed a great love for Jewish tradition, the same tradition that is practiced by Jews to this day. What if we could prove from ancient sources that the Jewish world of scholarship in his time was divided into two Schools, that the scholars in control of the community at the time he preached were of the School he opposed, and that the leading Torah sages of his century later referred to that same group he opposed as being "children of the devil" or considered them worthy of death?

The thesis I have proposed is based on the writings of the great Talmudist and anti-Shabbatean Rabbi Jacob Emden, a valiant champion of Orthodox Judaism during the eighteenth century.

His adversaries at the time were the Shabbateans, or followers of the false seventeenth century messiah, Shabbetai Zevi. These Shabbateans—or Frankists as they were called in his day—desecrated Jewish law and openly practiced sexual immorality. When excommunicated by the Polish rabbinate, they complained to certain Catholic bishops of being persecuted by the Jews because they believed in the Trinity. This eventually led to the burning of the Talmud in Poland, and these Frankists even tried to revive the notorious blood-libel against the Jews. When the leading rabbis of Poland asked Rabbi Emden whether it would be permitted to explain the true nature of these immoral heretics to the Polish authorities, Rabbi Emden replied in the affirmative, and also advised them to ask the Christians for help against the Shabbateans. This led him into a thorough analysis of the origins of Christianity and the original intent of its founders. He concluded that Jesus and Paul had intended to create a religion for the Gentiles based upon the seven Noahide Commandments. According to the Talmud and Tosefta, those Gentiles who observe these Commandments are considered of the Hasidim (pious ones) of the Nations, and merit a share in the World to Come. (The basic seven Noahide Commandments consist of the prohibitions against idolatry, blasphemy, stealing, murder, sexual sins, eating the limb of a living animal [cruelty to animals], and the imperative to establish courts of justice.) He believed that Jesus of Nazareth acted entirely according to the Halakha, and "brought about a double kindness to the world."[2] R. Emden stressed that Jesus spoke out strongly on behalf of the Torah of Moses, which indeed grants salvation to those Gentiles who practice the Noahide Commandments. R. Emden referred to Paul as "a scholar, an attendant of Rabban Gamaliel the Elder."

Returning now to the first century C.E., we know that two different schools of rabbinic authority existed at that time, Bet Shammai and Bet Hillel. These two schools are on record in the Mishnah and Talmud as having clashed on over three hundred and fifty occasions during the century they existed (about 30 B.C.E. to 70 C.E.). Nor were these minor controversies; they reached rather to the very heart of Judaism and its perspective on the world at large. The Talmud tells us (Sanhedrin 88B) that as the disciples of Shammai and Hillel increased, "the Torah became as two Torahs"; in other words, Judaism became split into two opposing approaches to its religious traditions.[3] And, very importantly for our subject, they were strongly at odds over Judaism's view of the Gentile world.

In previous chapters, I have pointed to Talmudic evidence that the Essenes—the apparent authors of the Dead Sea Scrolls[4]—were closely allied with the School of Hillel, and that Hillel and his disciples as well as the Essenes were referred to in the Talmud (Sanhedrin 11A *et al.*) as Hasidim (not Pharisees or Scribes).

We now know on the basis of the Dead Sea Scrolls that Jesus and Paul must have had some contact with these Essene Hasidim, as many parallel passages have been found in the Scrolls and the Christian Bible. Hundreds of similar passages (and many customs as well) have been found, and the Scrolls have been demonstrated through scientific process to be of an earlier date. Two important works on the subject are *The Scrolls and the New Testament* by K. Stendahl, and *The Ancient Library of Qumran* by Frank M. Cross. Many other excellent studies have been published.

We further noted that according to the Talmud (Sanhedrin 57A) and Maimonides (*Melakhim,* ch. 8), Moses obligated the Jews to spread knowledge of the Noahide Commandments to all mankind; therefore, when the Essenes gave their *raison d'être* as (Manual of Discipline) "to do what is good and upright before Him, as He has commanded through Moses . . . to love all the sons of light," we expressed our belief that they had such a mission to the Gentiles in mind.[5] We should take note here of one of the many parallel passages between the Scrolls and the Gospels. Jesus preached to his listeners (John 12:36): "While ye have the light, believe on the light, that ye may become sons of light."[6] Paul of Tarsus wrote similarly in his Epistle to the Ephesians (5:8): "Walk, then, as children of light." Hillel, founder of the school that bears his name (died about 10 C.E.), charged his disciples—and all Jews today follow the teachings of Bet Hillel—to be one who "loves mankind, and brings them nigh to the Torah" (Avot 1:12).[7]

We further expressed our belief, based on Talmudic sources, that when the School of Shammai gained control of the Jewish community (probably about 20 B.C.E.), the disciples of Hillel and of his assistant Menahem left to join the Essenes,[8] and to lead them in establishing a religion for the Gentiles.[9] It was then from the midst of these Essene Hasidim and disciples of Hillel that Jesus of Nazareth emerged on his mission.

Even prior to the Scrolls' discovery, many scholars suspected a link between the Essenes and Christianity. Thus, Robert Travers Herford writes in his piece on the Essenes in the *Universal Jewish Encyclopedia* (1941) that they were "concealing under a veil of secrecy a mystery of some kind. . . . They may have done so (contributed to the origin and growth of the Christian Church); but there is no positive evidence that they did, and no obvious reason why they should have." Perhaps we now have the evidence in the form of the Scrolls, and the reason would be Moses' obligation to spread knowledge of the Noahide Commandments to all mankind.

The French historian Ernest Renan also wrote in the nineteenth century, "Christianity is an Essenism which has largely succeeded." E. Schuré, author of *Les Grands Initiés,* believed that Jesus had been initiated into the secret doctrines of the Essenes. On the basis of such remarks and the Scrolls' discovery, Edmund Wilson—and he has been followed by others—wrote in his best-seller *The Scrolls From the Dead Sea* "that the rise of Christianity should, at last, be generally understood as simply an episode of human history rather than propagated as dogma and divine revelation." However, R. Jacob Emden's thesis that Jesus wished to spread knowledge of the ancient Noahide Commandments to the Gentiles brings the Essenes in as further proof that, as R. Jacob Emden held, Christianity was established entirely according to Jewish law (*"hakol al pi din v'dat torateinu"*).

(Stendahl's book contains an article by Nahum Glatzer, exploring various similarities between the teachings of Hillel and the Essenes, especially the oft-found common usage of the term "hesed." In Chapter Three I expressed my view—based on evidence from the Talmuds and the Scrolls—that Hillel was an Essene, and probably also a Teacher of Righteousness [*Moreh Tzedek*] of the group. See Talmud [Bava Batra 3B] where it is mentioned that Herod slew all the rabbis when he came to power, with the exception of Bava ben Buta, whom he blinded. The Tosafists [*ibid.*] declare that this account cannot be accepted literally, since the Sons of Bathyra—who served as *Nasi* before Hillel—and Hillel served in rabbinic office at the time. However, we know from Josephus that Herod held the Essenes in high esteem [Menahem, who was initially Hillel's *Av Bet Din,* was an Essene who had foretold Herod's rise to power], and Hillel's affiliation with the Essenes would explain why he was spared. As for the Sons of Bathyra, see Ta'anit 3A where it is recorded that the later R. Joshua ben Bathyra—of the same family—was called Son of Bathyra before his ordination. We may assume from this tradition that the Sons of Bathyra of Hillel's time were similarly not ordained rabbis. This would explain Herod's sparing them, as well as their lack of scholarship which led to Hillel's appointment [Pesahim 66A].)

The authors of the Damascus Document, found in the Essene caves at Qumran, bore a strong animosity toward the Pharisees of Bet Shammai.[10] They referred to them as traitors (*bogdim*) and "men of war." This scroll contains a prophecy foretelling that the followers of Bet Shammai will come to an end at about the time of the Temple's destruction. (We should assume that Jesus of Nazareth knew the contents of this Scroll well.)

Following the Temple's destruction (70 C.E.), the School of Hillel began to gain ascendancy over the School of Shammai. Bet Hillel's strength grew progressively until a Heavenly Voice (*bat kol*) was heard in Yavneh, [11] proclaiming that the Halakha was to be universally accepted in their favor. (This would have taken place some time toward the end of the first century C.E.) The later rabbis declared (Berakhot 36B), "The opinion of Bet Shammai when it conflicts with that of Bet Hillel is no Mishnah." In other words, their views were to be considered null and void.

But the Talmudic sages went further than the Heavenly Voice. They declared (Berakhot 11A): "He who observes the teachings of Bet Shammai deserves death." And lest one interpret this as a minor exaggeration, the Mishnah (Berakhot 10B) tells of an instance where a late first century C.E. sage, R. Tarfon, while on a journey, once observed a ruling of Bet Shammai with regard to the daily prayers; this sage later recounted that he had been set upon at the time by robbers, and the rabbis told him that he would have deserved to lose his life for having followed Bet Shammai's opinion.[12]

It would perhaps be worthwhile at this point to demonstrate how statements of Jesus, which were originally in-

tended as attacks on Bet Shammai, have been misinterpreted
and turned against the Jewish people as a whole, who—as Jesus himself foretold—have nullified the teachings of Shammai's School.

We might first refer to Jesus' rebuke to the Pharisees
(John 8:44): "You are of your father the devil, and your will
is to do your father's desires." This is echoed elsewhere, as,
for example (Revelation 2:9, 3:9), "the synagogue of Satan."
This has led to much anti-semitism, as well as Church decrees
against Jews. No one seems to have noticed that the first century C.E. Sage Dosa ben Harkinas, criticizing his brother Jonathan for having ruled in accordance with Bet Shammai in an
important case concerning levirate marriage, calls him "the
first-born of Satan" (Yevamot 16A). In other words, the rabbis of the first century C.E. were accustomed to refer to the
Pharisees of Bet Shammai as descendants of, or followers of,
the devil.[13]

A second example would be Jesus' statement (Matthew
5:38) "You have heard the commandment 'an eye for an eye,
a tooth for a tooth . . .' " which has led the Church to criticize
Jews as vengeful, cruel people. The Jewish community has
protested for centuries that we interpret this passage as call-
ing for monetary compensation, but to no avail; the Church
insists it has a tradition whereby the Pharisees of Jesus' time
interpreted "an eye for an eye" literally. Here again, I have
found no one pointing out that R. Eliezer is the only sage on
record (Bava Kamma 84A) as ruling that "an eye for an eye"
is to be interpreted literally, and R. Eliezer was known never
to deviate from the teachings of Bet Shammai (Shabbat 130B
and Niddah 7B).[14]

Before moving on to demonstrate that Jesus' well-known
attack on the Pharisees (Matthew 23)—which has caused so
much anti-semitism and persecution over the centuries—was
directed against the School of Shammai, we must first study

the different attitudes of the two Schools toward non-Jews. (A shorter study of Matthew 23 has already appeared in Chapter Four, note 14.) This would include not only the views of Bet Hillel and Bet Shammai themselves, but also the opinions of the two leading sages during the latter part of the first century C.E., R. Joshua and R. Eliezer—the former recognized as a firm adherent of Bet Hillel,[15] the latter as a diehard follower of Bet Shammai. We shall also have to examine the evident link between Bet Shammai and the Zealot party (*Kanna'im* or *Beryoni*)[16] in the early part of the first century C.E.

1. The Talmud (Shabbat 31A) relates that three heathens appeared before Shammai and Hillel for the purpose of conversion, but each of them harbored reservations about various aspects of Judaism. Shammai rebuffed them, but Hillel reasoned patiently with all three, ultimately winning their confidence and allegiance. The differing views of the two sages toward the three heathens has been examined at length in Chapter Two. (The passing of the "eighteen measures" by the School of Shammai, which were in the main designed to cause greater separation between Jews and Gentiles, also apparently took place during the lifetimes of Hillel and Shammai [see Shabbat 17A, Tosefta Shabbat 1:8 and Tosafists, Shabbat 14B, bottom].)

2. R. Joshua maintained that the pious amongst the Gentiles merit a share in the World to Come. Since the only laws incumbent upon Gentiles according to Judaism are the Noahide Commandments, their observance is understood. R. Eliezer, the Shammaite, held that no Gentile merited a share in the World to Come, no matter how pious or righteous he might be (Sanhedrin 105A; Tosefta, Sanhedrin ch. 13). (See Chapter Two where I demonstrated that Hillel and Shammai themselves debated this issue.)

3. Aquila the proselyte, a scholarly convert to Judaism who translated the Bible into Greek, is recorded as having

held a conversation with R. Eliezer and R. Joshua over what rank a convert might aspire to in the community of sages. R. Eliezer told him that the convert has no place amongst them,[17] and Aquila, as a result, was ready to desert Judaism and revert to paganism (he had been a relative of Hadrian). R. Joshua then assured him that he was a full member of the Torah community, and he was thus consoled and strengthened in his devotion to Judaism (Midrash Genesis Rabbah 70:5).

As for the relationship of Bet Shammai with the Zealot party—which Josephus called a "fourth philosophy" (after the Pharisees, Essenes and Sadducees)—the Zealots were founded (reorganized? see later) in 6 C.E. by Judah the Galilean and Zadok the Pharisee (Josephus, Antiquities 18:1–10). The Zealots' hatred of the Romans and all Gentiles was surely the common bond that aligned them with Bet Shammai. Josephus' mention of Zadok the Pharisee is the conclusive proof of their alliance, for there is no record of any other Zadok at that time amongst the Pharisees except the one mentioned in Talmudic sources as a member of Bet Shammai (Yevamot 15B; Tosefta Eduyyot 2:2. The identification of Zadok the Pharisee mentioned by Josephus as the Sage by the same name of Bet Shammai is confirmed by A. Hyman [*Toledot Tanna'im* 1:201], the historian Graetz, the *Jewish Encyclopedia* [3:115 and 12:641–642] and the *Universal Jewish Encyclopedia* 2:251). Josephus described the Zealots' atrocities against the Jewish community, branded them as common murderers and robbers, and blamed them for the Temple's destruction. The Talmud too calls the Zealots murderers (Mishnah, Sotah 47A), recounts how they burned down the storehouses of food in Jerusalem in order to prevent the Jews from negotiating a peaceful settlement with the Romans (Gittin 56A), and blamed the destruction of the Temple on R. Zechariah ben

Avkulot, a priest-Pharisee who would not allow the sacrifice of an offering sent by the Roman emperor, even though the Rabbis had permitted it (*ibid.*)—this R. Zechariah, according to scholars, being identified by Josephus as a Zealot leader.[18] The two important points to remember are (1) that both the Talmud and Josephus called these Zealots "murderers" and (2) their direct connection with Bet Shammai.

Josephus' hatred and derision of the Zealots really needs no further elaboration here. He refers to them throughout his works as robbers and murderers (see Wars 2:13, par. 2 and 3). He seems to sum up his feelings toward the end of his work (Wars 7:8, 269–273): "For they imitated every wicked work; nor if history suggested any evil thing that had formerly been done, did they avoid zealously to do the same. . . . It was impossible they could be punished according to their deserving." We should note that these words were written immediately prior to his account of Masada, and he surely intended them so that the reader would not sympathize with the Zealots as they met their Waterloo. The historian often noted that they sought to advance their own ambitions, rather than those of the nation, and that they murdered large numbers of innocent people. It is highly probable that the Masada incident was omitted from the Talmud for this reason.

Josephus makes quite clear his feelings that by waging their war with the Romans, and obstructing any negotiations with them, the Zealots were to blame for the destruction of the Temple. This corresponds with the Talmud's picture of them (Gittin 56A).

Scholars have in fact raised a contradiction in Josephus, for the historian states (Antiquities 18:1–10) that the Zealots were founded by Judah the Galilean and Zadok the Pharisee in 6 C.E., yet he records elsewhere (Wars 1:204) that Hezekiah established the group several decades earlier. It is probable, however, that Josephus is telling us that under Judah and Zadok a more formal alliance was forged between Zealots and Pharisees, the latter being Bet Shammai.

Another example of the Bet Shammai-Zealot connection appears in the person of Eleazar ben Hananiah, a leading priest shortly before the Temple's destruction. (We discussed his father Hananiah ben Hezekiah in Chapter Three.) Josephus (Wars 2:409) identifies him as a Zealot leader who refused to accept gifts or sacrifices for the Temple from the Romans or any foreigner, and he is also quoted in the Mekhilta (Exodus 20:8) as concurring with Shammai on a ruling concerning preparations for the Sabbath.

Josephus also records that the Zealots fought with no regard for the Sabbath, and even slew a group of surrendering Romans on that day (Wars 2:449–456). Permission for waging a war in progress even on the Sabbath is a ruling of Shammai (Shabbat 19A); could the Zealots have asked him for a decision?

As for Bet Hillel's view of the Zealots, R. Johanan ben Zakkai of Bet Hillel sought to negotiate with the Romans despite the Zealots' objection (Gittin 56A). According to the Midrash (Kohelet Rabbah 7:11), these terrorists sought to assassinate him. R. Gamaliel the Elder, grandson of Hillel, is quoted in Acts of the Apostles (5:37) as strongly denigrating Judas the Galilean, a founder of the Zealots.

One further observation. One of the first debates between Bet Shammai and Bet Hillel concerned the so-called "eighteen measures" (Shabbat 13B), which Bet Shammai sought to introduce as a means of creating further separation between Jews and Gentiles. Bet Hillel opposed these measures, and the Jerusalem Talmud records (Shabbat 1:4) that during the course of the debate, an unspecified number of Bet Hillel's members were murdered by Bet Shammai (strong evidence exists that Zealots were present at the time, and I believe it was they who did the actual killing; see Chapter Three). Many of Hillel's disciples—some of whom were killed that day—are referred to in the Talmud as prophets (Sukkah 28A and Bava Batra 134A).[19]

Having acquainted ourselves with these important facts, we may now attempt to fathom Jesus' great attack on the Pharisees (Matthew 23), and demonstrate how it was directed against Bet Shammai, who were then in control of the rabbinic community. Jesus first accuses them, "You shut up the kingdom of heaven in men's faces," and then describes them as "You who travel over sea and land to make a single proselyte." Because of these views he accuses them of being "hypocrites."

The first accusation would refer to Bet Shammai's position—as per R. Eliezer (Sanhedrin 105A)—that no Gentile merits a share in the World to Come, even those who observe the Noahide Commandments. At the same time, Shammai discouraged the acceptance of proselytes to Judaism (Shabbat 31A), and this explains Jesus' second charge. By maintaining such views, the School of Shammai made it virtually impossible for even the most sincere and virtuous Gentile to find his way to salvation. It would have certainly been impossible and even heretical to found a religion such as Christianity—based on the Noahide Commandments and the promise of everlasting life to pious Gentiles—according to Bet Shammai. This led to Jesus' charge that they were "hypocrites," and that "you have rejected the weightier matters of the Law—justice, mercy, good faith." The Kabbalists have in fact identified the School of Hillel—who disagreed with Bet Shammai on both of these issues—as emanating from the sphere of *Hesed* or "mercy" (Zohar, Ra'aya Meheimna 3:245A).

Jesus also criticizes Bet Shammai's treatment of proselytes ("and when you have him . . ."), as we have already noted in R. Eliezer's attitude toward the scholarly convert Aquila, who almost reverted to Paganism because of Bet Shammai's position.

Jesus of Nazareth then introduces a most serious charge against these Pharisees. He quotes them as saying, "We would never have joined in shedding the blood of the prophets, had we lived in our fathers' day." The debate over the "eighteen measures," at which time a number of Hillel's disciples, identified in the Talmud as "prophets," were killed, would have taken place about 20 to 10 B.C.E., or a half century before 30 C.E., when Jesus spoke these words. The members of Bet Shammai present at the debate would have been the fathers of the Pharisees he was now attacking. These Pharisees claimed they would not have done as their fathers (whether it was Bet Shammai themselves, or their allies, the Zealots, who did the actual killing). But, he continues, "Your own evidence tells against you! You are the sons of those who murdered the prophets!" He is referring here to the fact that R. Zadok—a leader of Bet Shammai—joined forces with the Zealot chief Judah the Galilean in 6 C.E., thus proving that they followed in their fathers' footsteps by aligning themselves with these murderers and assassins.[20] (This R. Zadok began a forty year fast in 30 C.E. so that the Temple might not be destroyed. It was probably at that time that he began practicing according to the teaching of Bet Hillel [Yevamot 15B].)

Jesus then accuses these Pharisees of murdering Zechariah ben Berechia ("whom you murdered . . .") in the Temple. Julius Wellhausen and other scholars have connected this accusation with Josephus' account of the murder of a righteous man named Zechariah ben Berechia on the Temple grounds by the Zealots (Wars 4:335). A major objection to Wellhausen's interpretation has been that Jesus is speaking here to the Pharisees, and not to Zealots. However, since we have established a direct link between Bet Shammai and the Zealots, Wellhausen may be vindicated.[21]

The most impressive proof for my interpretation is the similarity between Jesus' criticism and the Talmudic Sages' statements concerning Bet Shammai (toward the close of the first century C.E., after the Heavenly Voice's intervention against them). Jesus says, "You will draw down on yourselves the blood of every holy man that has been shed on earth." The Talmudic Sages said (Berakhot 11A and Jerusalem Talmud, Berakhot 1:4): "He who observes the teachings of Bet Shammai deserves death." And when the Sage R. Tarfon acted according to Bet Shammai in one instance, the Sages told him (Mishnah, Berakhot 10B) that he deserved to be killed.

I must however stress again my personal view that Bet Shammai themselves were not involved in the murders of the members of Bet Hillel, but were criticized for having aligned themselves as the intellectual sponsors of the Zealot terrorists. What had united them, of course, was their common hatred of the Gentile world, personified by their Roman oppressors.

I should like to list here additional support for my contention that Jesus was attacking Bet Shammai only, and not Bet Hillel.

He begins by exhorting his listeners to do all the Pharisees command them, since "they occupy the chair of Moses." Bet Hillel accepted the rulings of Bet Shammai when the latter constituted a majority. However, Bet Shammai did not view Bet Hillel's decisions as binding even when the latter constituted a majority, as they considered themselves intellectually superior (Yevamot 14A). He thus identifies himself as a follower of Bet Hillel.

Jesus also describes these Pharisees as "straining out gnats, and swallowing camels," a clear reference to Bet Shammai, who were "sharper" (*ibid.*). (Anti-semites often speak of

Jews as being shrewd and practicing casuistry. Is this their source?)

Jesus further states concerning these Pharisees that "they tie up heavy burdens and lay them on men's shoulders," again a clear reference to Bet Shammai, who almost always adopted a more stringent opinion than Bet Hillel.

He also declares that these Pharisees liked to be called Rabbi,[22] and reminds his listeners that he who humbles himself shall be exalted. This appears to be a direct reference to a Talmudic passage (Eruvin 13B) which describes the humble members of Bet Hillel as always reciting the opinion of Bet Shammai before their own in the House of Study. The Talmud (*ibid.*) gives Bet Hillel's humility as the reason the Halakha was eventually accepted in their favor. In this well-known statement, Jesus is actually expressing his hope for the return of Bet Hillel to power.

Shortly prior to the attack on the Pharisees, we read in the Christian Bible how some Pharisees got together to disconcert Jesus (Matthew 22). We seem to recognize them as the same disciples of Bet Shammai who grouped together against Hillel at the Temple (Betsah 20A), as well as against one of his disciples (*ibid.*, 20B). There is no record anywhere of a member of Bet Hillel acting in such fashion.[23]

We should also point out here that, contrary to many Christians' thinking, the Talmudic literature does not contain criticism of Jesus. Some have sought to link him with a Yeshua Hanotzri, who is said to have practiced magic and sought to lead Israel astray (Sotah 47A and Sanhedrin 107B, but censored in contemporary texts). But a foremost historian of the rabbinate, the twelfth century Abraham ibn Daud, wrote (*Sefer Ha-Kabbalah*, Jewish Publication Society Edition, p. 15) that we possess a true tradition (*Kabalat Emet*) that this Yeshua Hanotzri lived during the reign of Alexander Yannai (died 76 B.C.E.), and had been a disciple of Joshua ben Perachiah, thus making it impossible for him to have been the founder of Christianity. This tradition is also given by Nahmanides (*Vikuakh Ha-Ramban,* Mossad edition, p. 306). R. Jehiel Heilprin, the seventeenth century rabbinic historian, lists two Yeshua Hanotzris, the first being the earlier controversial disciple of Joshua ben Perachiah who lived during Yannai's reign, and the second as the founder of Christianity (*Seder Hadorot,* pp. 147, 148 and 151).

Some have tried to link Jesus with a magician named Ben Stada, but R. Jacob Tam—the eminent Tosafist and grandson of Rashi—dismissed this (Shabbat 104B), as he had lived during the second century.

This same R. Jacob Tam recorded (Sanhedrin 63B and Bekhorot 2B) that Trinitarianism is permitted to Gentiles, even though it is considered an idolatrous act if practiced by a Jew.

Unfortunately, many people—and especially those possessing an anti-semitic frame of mind—have had a field-day with Jesus' attack on the Pharisees. One can only guess at how many pogroms and persecutions were instigated against Jews because of this misinterpretation. Such actions have not only caused terrible harm to innocent men, women and children, but also maligned the memory of the Founder of Christianity amongst his own people.[24]

The Christian Bible (Matthew 24) portrays Jesus as brooding over the imminent destruction of the Temple and Jerusalem, quoting at the same time from the Book of Daniel. It seems quite clear that he believed that his mission might have averted the impending doom, as he laments (Luke 19) "because thou hast not known the time of thy visitation." This would have taken place in 30 C.E., the year of his death, or forty years prior to the destruction of the Temple in 70 C.E. We have, on the basis of R. Jacob Emden's writings, identified his mission as that of creating a religion for the Gentiles based on the Noahide Commandments, according to the Halakha. It therefore behooves us to examine the reasons given by the Rabbis for the destruction of the Temple in 70 C.E., and the ill-boding signs that began appearing in 30 C.E.

The Talmud states (Nazir 32B) that although Jewish tradition could not identify the day of the Temple's destruction, the year was known as 70 C.E. on the basis of Daniel's prophecy (Daniel 9:24). The Talmud further tells us (Yoma 39B) that in the year 30 C.E. the doors of the Temple Sanctuary would open by themselves (as a sign to admit the enemy: Rashi),[25] until R. Johanan ben Zakkai rebuked them, saying, "Sanctuary, Sanctuary, why wilt thou be the alarmer thyself?" The Sage then quotes a prophecy from Zechariah (11:1), giving this as the sign of the Temple's impending destruction. The Talmud (*ibid.*) cites three additional omens taking place in 30 C.E., and related to the Temple service, as pointing to its doom.[26] Thus, in 30 C.E., the Sages—particularly Bet Hillel's R. Johanan ben Zakkai—realized that the end was approaching.

Why was the Second Temple destroyed? What was it that had kindled God's wrath against his Sanctuary? The only tradition given in all major rabbinic sources—the Babylonian Talmud (Yoma 9B), the Jerusalem Talmud (Yoma 1:1) and Tosefta (end Menahot)—is the existence of "hatred without cause" among the people. However, neither Talmud spells out the nature of this "hatred," nor to whom it was directed. We should therefore quote and translate from the Tosefta (*ibid.*), where an explanation is offered: ". . . each one hated his fellow man. This is to teach you that hatred of one's fellow man is severely judged by God, and is considered as serious an offense as idolatry, adultery and murder combined. But in the final (Third) Temple, may it be built during our lifetimes, what is written? (Isaiah 2) 'And it shall come to pass in the last days that the Mountain of the Lord's House shall be established in the top of the mountains . . . and many peoples shall go and say, Come ye, and let us go up to the Mountain of the Lord, to the House of the God of Jacob . . .' and it is further written (Jeremiah 31) 'For there shall be a day, that the watchmen upon the Mount Ephraim shall cry, Arise ye, and let us go up to Zion unto the Lord our God.' "

The Tosefta's message is quite clear; the "hatred without cause" was the hatred of the Jews toward the Gentile world.[27] The teachings of Bet Hillel, such as 'Love mankind, and bring them nigh to the Torah,' were not practiced by the people. In the year 30 C.E., the Pharisees were controlled by Bet Shammai, and the Sanhedrin was dominated by Bet Shammai, the Zealots and violent Temple priests (see Pesahim 57A). Hillel had died about 10 C.E., virtually all of his disciples had left to join the Essenes, and the people—probably in the main because of their Roman conquerors—turned with great hatred toward the Gentile world.[28]

This then was obviously the goal of Jesus, and—as we have mentioned many times in this book—the Essenes and the disciples of Hillel as well, for it was from their midst that he emerged. If we could only show the Almighty that we still possessed a love for all mankind in our hearts, so that Jews would continue to observe the Torah, and Gentiles would be brought the message of salvation through observance of the Noahide Laws, as passed down from Moses at Sinai—Jew and Gentile, both according to their own practice, with brotherhood and love in their hearts, in the Temple at Jerusalem—perhaps then the Almighty would cancel the decree foreseen by the prophets.

But it was not meant to be so; and the House of our God perished in flames.

THE PROPHET ELIJAH
CONDEMNS THE CRUCIFIXION

It is difficult to write about the crucifixion of Jesus. Rivers of Jewish blood have been shed because of it, despite the fact that it was Romans, and not Jews, who performed the execution. But the Gospels insist that a Jewish Sanhedrin delivered him up to the Romans, after adjudging him guilty. The most enigmatic aspect of all this is that scholars have been unable to ascertain with any degree of precision the cause of the guilt. Some have suggested blasphemy, others that he claimed to be the Messiah, but all such theories lack substance when scrutinized in the light of Jewish law.[29]

I should like to suggest a different approach based on R. Jacob Emden's thesis that Jesus of Nazareth had sought to establish a religion for the Gentiles based upon the Noahide Commandments. The Christian Bible tells us (John 11:49–51; 18:14) that the High Priest Caiaphas, who had convened the Sanhedrin to try Jesus, said to them, "It is better for one man to die for the people, than for the whole nation to be destroyed." This phrase is found virtually verbatim in one rabbinic source (Midrash Genesis Rabbah 94:9) in conjunction with a Halakhic ruling which was discussed some two hundred years after Jesus' crucifixion. We shall seek to demonstrate that this later case bears a direct relationship to Caiaphas' remark and the resultant crucifixion.

The Halakha under discussion there states (Tosefta, Terumot 7:23) that if a group of traveling Jews are suddenly confronted by Gentiles who demand that they hand over a Jew to them to be killed, or else they will all be murdered, they must all agree to die and not hand over one of their number. However, if the Gentiles identify a specific Jew to be handed over, he should be given to them. It is then related (Jerusalem

Talmud, Terumot, end ch. 8, and Midrash Genesis Rabbah 94:9) that a certain Ulla bar Koshev—apparently a member of the rabbinic community—was once sentenced to death by the Romans, and he sought protection at the home of the third century C.E. Sage R. Joshua ben Levi. Representatives of the Romans soon appeared in the town, and threatened to kill a large number of Jews if Ulla was not turned over to them. The Jerusalem Talmud records that the Sage then spoke to Ulla, convinced him to surrender, and handed him over to the Romans. But the Midrash is more explicit, and quotes R. Joshua as uttering basically the same words spoken two hundred years earlier by Caiaphas, "It is better that you should die than that the community [30] should be punished because of you," and R. Joshua then handed him over to the Romans.

The Jerusalem Talmud and the Midrash then tell us that R. Joshua ben Levi had previously been frequently visited by the prophet Elijah (according to the Talmuds, exemplary pious sages were accorded this honor), but the Prophet ceased visiting him following this incident. R. Joshua fasted for a long time, until Elijah finally appeared to him. Angrily, Elijah rebuked the Sage, "I do not visit those who hand over a Jew." R. Joshua replied in self-defense, "Did I not act in accordance with the Mishnah (teaching or law)?" Ulla had of course been identified by the Gentiles as the one causing the danger, and it was therefore permitted to surrender him in order to save the other lives. The Prophet again reprimanded him, "Is this the Mishnah of the Hasidim (pious ones)?" The usual interpretation here is that although R. Joshua had acted in accordance with the law, the Hasidim (truly pious) were expected to act beyond the letter of the law, and someone other than the sage should have handed Ulla over to the Romans.[31] However, this is difficult, especially as we do not find any precedent in Jewish law to differentiate between Hasidim and others where danger to life is involved.[32] (The Halakhic principle involved here is that of the *"rodef"* [pursuer], i.e., one who pursues an innocent person with the intent of killing him, any individual having the right and obligation to save the pursued innocent, even if it necessitates slaying the pursuer [see Sanhedrin 72B–74A].)[33]

Since we have established that the formula spoken by Caiaphas and R. Joshua ben Levi pertained to the same Halakha, I believe there is a more profound analogy here. I have expressed my opinion many times in this book that Christianity as a religion for the Gentiles was founded by the Hasidim—the Essenes and disciples of Hillel from whose midst Jesus of Nazareth emerged. I have also demonstrated that the Pharisees criticized by Jesus were the School of Shammai, who dominated Jewish life and thought in Jesus' time, and therefore were the Pharisees in control of Caiaphas' Sanhedrin as well. Bet Shammai would have been opposed to Christianity on two grounds. First, they held salvation of the Gentiles to be impossible, for, according to them, even those Gentiles who observed the Noahide Commandments did not merit a share in the World to Come, as per R. Eliezer (Sanhedrin 105A). The only mitigating factor would have been that such a Gentile religion might have helped the Jews—especially in the long exile foretold by the prophets, which was soon to begin. Perhaps Rome's conversion to Christianity might even have saved the Jerusalem Temple, as the Romans would have been brought closer to the Torah of Moses. But Bet Shammai's negative attitude toward the Gentiles would have dismissed such a stance. They would have argued that if the pagans received a new religion based on the Torah of Moses, it would only be a matter of time before they would insist that theirs was the only true religion, that Jews be missionized, and even persecuted and forced to embrace their new faith. A "new covenant" to the Gentiles would come to mean a breaking with the old, rather than a strengthening and reaffirmation.[34] According to Bet Shammai, such a new religion would not lead to brotherhood under God, but to the murder and persecution of Jews.[35]

We may now attempt to comprehend the session of the Sanhedrin as recorded in John (11:47). The priests and Pharisees said, "If we let him go on like this, the whole world will believe in him. Then the Romans will come in and sweep away our Sanctuary and our nation." In other words, they feared that if the Roman rulers should embrace Christianity, they would destroy the Temple and Jewish government. Caiaphas then pointed out to them that the main issue was not the Temple or government, but Jewish lives! Christians would murder Jews! Jesus would have then been accounted as a "pursuer" (*rodef*) of the innocent under Jewish law, and it was for this reason that he was sentenced to death.

Needless to say, the Hasidim—Bet Hillel and the Essenes—held a different view of the Gentile world. Hillel had taught "Love mankind and bring them nigh to the Torah," and the Essenes had given as their goal "to love all the sons of light."[36] R. Joshua ben Hananiah of Bet Hillel gave their tradition (Sanhedrin 105A)—which is accepted by all Jewry since the Heavenly Voice's intervention in favor of Bet Hillel—that those Gentiles who observe the Noahide Commandments merit a share in the World to Come. To them the Gentiles were not a threat, and certainly not murderers. To the Hasidim, the Gentiles would become brothers in God's Kingdom. I would venture to say therefore that Jesus of Nazareth was mainly motivated by just such a hope: that the conversion of Rome to Christianity—according to the Noahide Commandments of the Torah of Moses—would save the Temple.

Bet Hillel's Relationship With Early Christianity

With regard to Bet Hillel's relationship with early Christianity, attention should here be drawn to R. Gamaliel the
Elder's intervention in order to save the lives of the Apostles,
after they had been sentenced to death by the Sanhedrin
(Acts 5:34). In his statement to the latter body—which is recorded in the Acts of the Apostles (5:39)—this grandson of
Hillel states, "If it (Christianity) does in fact come from God
you will not only be unable to destroy them, but you might
find yourselves fighting against God." (See R. Jacob Emden's
comment in *Lechem Shamayim* to Avot 4:11, where he refers to
Christianity and Islam as an "assembly for the sake of
Heaven" which will in the end be established.) R. Gamaliel
thereby offers a strong indication that he knew what the ultimate purpose of its founder was—namely, as a religion for
the Gentiles according to the Halakha.

Can it then be ascribed solely to coincidence that only several chapters later (Acts 9), Paul, a disciple of R. Gamaliel,
emerges as the Apostle to the Gentiles? Paul spoke with pride
of his studies under the Sage (Acts 22). I have also previously
pointed out (see Chapter Four) that the Jewish-Christians
who initially opposed Paul and refused to admit uncircumcised Gentiles into the Christian Church were influenced by
the teachings of certain Pharisees who had joined them (Acts
15:5); we now understand that those Pharisees were Shammaites who would have given their School's position that even
those Gentiles who observe the Noahide Commandments do
not merit a share in the World to Come, and this position
caused the error of the Apostles. Paul, like Jesus before him,
had ties to Bet Hillel, and knew the Hillelite view that righteous Gentiles merit salvation. Accordingly, Paul's statements
concerning Jews must also be viewed within the same context
of protest against Bet Shammai's influence in his time.

Jewish scholars have long been mystified as to why Simeon—son of Hillel and father of R. Gamaliel the Elder—who served as Nasi following Hillel's death, is not quoted or discussed even once in the entire Talmudic literature (except for the brief statement that he succeeded Hillel [Shabbat 15A]). I believe that the Talmud is thereby telling us that the School of Hillel reached its nadir in his time, and that he had no say at all in the affairs of the community.

Elijah Condemns Caiaphas and His Sanhedrin

Returning now to the Jerusalem Talmud and Midrash, we realize that R. Joshua ben Levi is not recorded as having approached the Romans in an attempt to save Ulla's life. If he would have spoken to them as a rabbi of God's love for humanity, of man being created in the image of God, or similar teachings, perhaps they would have relented and spared Ulla. He made no attempt however to plead with the Romans. The Prophet Elijah thus rebuked R. Joshua ben Levi for uttering Caiaphas' words and handing over a Jew. When R. Joshua replied that he had acted within the law, the Prophet reminded him that this was not "*Mishnat Ha-Hasidim,* that a true Hasid would have first endeavored to speak to the Gentiles, to intervene and attempt to teach and inspire them. A Hasid had to see the best in humanity. Since R. Joshua had not acted in such a manner, he was not worthy of the Prophet's visitation. Thus, Elijah's condemnation was in reality directed simultaneously toward Caiaphas and his Sanhedrin as well, for they too had handed over a Jew, and not judged the Gentiles as the Hasidim had.

The Jerusalem Talmud in fact gives the Prophet's rebuke as "Is this the Mishnah of the Hasidim?" to which the Midrash adds, "Such an act should have been carried out by others, and not by you." But here again the Midrash does not mean to imply that R. Joshua should have bowed out of the picture, while someone else surrendered Ulla. The Prophet is rather saying that some other person should have remained with Ulla, ready to hand him over at a later time should the Sage's mission to the Gentiles prove fruitless.

We should also note that after giving the Tosefta's ruling that the Jew identified by the Gentiles may be handed over— and immediately prior to the incident involving the Prophet Elijah—the Jerusalem Talmud records a dispute between the two third century C.E. Amoraim, R. Johanan and Resh Lakish. According to the latter, he may be handed over only if he is guilty of a capital offense according to the Torah, whereas R. Johanan rules that even a completely innocent person may be surrendered to the Gentiles. It is entirely possible then that Ulla bar Koshev was really an innocent man despite an unjust Roman conviction, and this led to the Prophet's condemnation (*Turei Zahav* [see note 32] initially offers this interpretation, but abandons it because he believes Maimonides to have assumed that Ulla was guilty of a crime). If this were so, two important questions before the Sanhedrin at Jesus' trial would have been, first, whether an innocent man may be handed over, and second, whether a mission to the Gentiles takes precedence. The term "Mishnah of the Hasidim" would then apply both to Resh Lakish's opinion (which would explain why Maimonides adopted his view, even though R. Johanan's opinion is always accepted)[37] and to the mission.

Our previous identification and analysis of the mission of the Hasidim to the Gentiles two centuries earlier has thus enabled us to offer this new understanding of the Prophet's reference to "Mishnah of the Hasidim."

It would seem that R. Judah Ha-Nasi—a descendant of Hillel in the second century C.E. who compiled the most important work of Jewish law, the Mishnah—left Bet Hillel's view of Caiaphas for posterity by referring to him (Parah 3:5) as *Ha-Kof* (the monkey), a play on his name[38] which would be related to his remark before the Sanhedrin.

NOTES

1. The twentieth century arch-enemy of the Jewish people, A. Hitler, did not neglect to stress this point (*Mein Kampf*, Houghton Mifflin, pp. 422–423): "Of course, the latter (Jesus) made no secret of his disposition toward the Jewish people, and when necessary he even took to the whip in order to drive out of the Lord's Temple this adversary of all humanity. . . ."

2. Rabbi Emden's reply to the Polish rabbinate—or Council of the Four Lands as it was known at the time—may be found in an appendix to his edition of the *Seder Olam* (1757), a Tannaitic historical work. He republished the letter in his *Sefer Shimmush* (1758–1762).

   I have recently translated the most pertinent portions of this document.

3. It should be stressed that the differences between the two Schools involved the oral traditions passed down from Moses and the Prophets, to be used in the interpretation of the written Torah (the Bible). It was forbidden to commit any part of these oral traditions to writing, nor the discussions of the rabbis concerning them. The first written version of the Oral Law appeared about 200 C.E. in the form of the Mishnah—edited by R. Judah Ha-Nasi, a descendant of Hillel—finally published out of fear that it might otherwise be forgotten.

   It is difficult for individuals of the twentieth century—accustomed as we are to books and libraries—to fully grasp this oral system. At the same time, it is fairly easy to recognize how it could eventually lead to contradictory opinions, and how the public at large might not have been privy to the intense controversies that simmered behind the walls of the first century yeshivot.

4. The *Halakhot Gedolot,* an eighth century C.E. Geonic work, states (*Hilkhot Soferim*) that the elders (original disciples) of Bet Shammai and Bet Hillel wrote the Scroll of the Hasmoneans, but it will not be found by future generations until the priest arises for the *Urim and Thummim* (a reference to the messianic age). *Halakhot Gedolot* also records that Bet Shammai and Bet Hillel wrote the Megillat Ta'anit (a scroll listing important and happy dates in early Jewish history which are forbidden to be observed as fast days) in the attic of Hananiah ben Hezekiah ben Garon, but a later rabbinic court placed it in a *Genizah* (hidden place).

R. David Luria, in the introduction to his edition of Pirkei D'Rabbi Eliezer (p. 12A), raises strong questions on both these statements. As for the Scroll of the Hasmoneans, he points out that if it is a reference to the Book of the Maccabees (or, as others believe, the Scroll of Antiochus), copies are extant nowadays! Regarding the Megillat Ta'anit tradition, he points out that we still possess it as well nowadays.

I should like to suggest that the traditions of the *Halakhot Gedolot* refer to the only *Genizah* (hiding place) we know of that existed in the first century B.C.E. and first century C.E., the era of the two Schools—namely, the caves of the Essene Hasidim at Qumran. We now know that literary documents of the ancient Israelites were stored there. With regard to the Megillat Ta'anit, both the Talmud (Shabbat 13B) and Halakhot Gedolot quote R. Simeon ben Gamaliel, a descendant of Hillel, as expressing opposition to it. I would therefore suggest that following the great debate between Bet Shammai and Bet Hillel over the "eighteen measures," at which time members of Bet Hillel were killed (see later in this chapter), a rabbinic court of Bet Hillel concealed this festal scroll at the *Genizah* (it should be noted that the date of this debate—the ninth of Adar—was observed as a fast day for centuries among Jews). Returning to Luria's first question, a first century B.C.E. manuscript of the Scroll of the Hasmoneans written by the two schools would have also remained at Qumran. The Halakhot Gedolot is therefore telling us that this Scroll—or, better stated, the entire *Gen-*

izah at Qumran—will not be found until the dawn of the Messianic Age.

5. In Chapter Three I noted that the phrase "good and upright" is probably a reference to Deuteronomy 6:18, which the Talmud interprets (Bava Mezia 16B) as acting beyond the letter of the law. It was for this reason that they were referred to as Hasidim, which denotes such observance of the Torah.

    It is clear from the Talmud (Sanhedrin 57A) and Maimonides (*Melakhim* ch. 8) that Moses obligated the Jews to spread knowledge of the Noahide Commandments to the Gentiles only from a position of strength, which they never achieved. Thus, the establishment of Christianity as a religion for the Gentiles by the Hasidim was an act above and beyond the requirements of Jewish law (*lifnim mi-shurat hadin*).

6. It is mentioned earlier in the same chapter of John (12:20) that a group of Greek Gentiles were present at the time in the Temple, and Jesus' remark was apparently directed toward them.

    Even if he was speaking to his fellow Jews, we realize now that Jesus of Nazareth wished them to return to the teachings of Bet Hillel (see Matthew 10, where he refers to "the lost sheep of Israel"); in this case, he could have been speaking to them as well. The Essenes expressly stated "all the sons of light," which would encompass both Jews and Gentiles, each according to their own practice.

7. See Chapter Five where we brought evidence from Avot D'Rabbi Nathan 12:7–8 that Hillel intended the Gentiles when he referred to "mankind" here.

    (Cf. Shabbat 88B where the Talmud states that every single word that went forth from the Omnipotent during the revelation at Sinai split up into seventy languages, i.e., it was given to all humanity. The Talmud derives this from Psalm 68 which reads "The Lord giveth the word; they that publish the tidings are a great host." Compare with John 1:1, "In the beginning was the word.")

8. The source for this is Hagigah 16B, where it is recorded that eighty pairs of disciples left the rabbinic community with Menahem the Essene (see Chapter Three). The only other refer-

ence to eighty pairs of disciples is found in the Jerusalem Talmud (Nedarim, end ch. 5), listing them as disciples of Hillel.

9. See Hagigah 16B where the departure of the eighty pairs of disciples along with Menahem is described by the Talmud as being "in the service of the king." The Jerusalem Talmud (Hagigah 2:2) further describes their exodus as a mission of conciliation to the Gentiles. (Cf. Chapter Three.)

R. Jehiel Heilprin (*Seder Hadorot*) identifies this Menahem as Menahem the Essene.

10. See Chapters Three and Six where I dwelled at length on this point.

11. The Heavenly Voice is mentioned in both Talmuds (Eruvin 13B and Berakhot 1:4). It proclaimed, "Both are the words of the living God, but the Halakha is as Bet Hillel."

12. Bertinoro and the commentary *Penei Moshe* to the Jerusalem Talmud interpret the Sages' admonition to R. Tarfon as "you deserved to be killed; and had you died, you would have been guilty for your soul." These last words either mean he would have brought about his own death, or that he sinned against his soul.

13. Rashi (Yevamot 16A) connects this with their exceptional shrewdness, as well as with their refusal to accede to Bet Hillel even when they knew they were wrong (i.e., when Bet Hillel constituted a majority, or following the Heavenly Voice's decree).

With regard to "Synagogues of Satan," it would be difficult to picture Bet Shammai and Bet Hillel as having prayed together in the same synagogues, as basic differences existed between them in both custom and liturgy. See for example the dispute concerning the daily reading of the *Shma* (Berakhot 10B), where Bet Shammai rule that it must be recited while standing in the morning and reclining in the evening, whereas Bet Hillel hold it may be read in any position. Another example would be the Tosefta (end Rosh Ha-Shanah), where a bitter exchange is recorded between the two Schools over the liturgy, should Rosh Ha-Shanah or a festival fall on the Sabbath.

14. See Bava Kamma 84A where the Talmud asks in apparent disbelief, "Can R. Eliezer disagree with all these sages?" The fourth century C.E. Amora Rabbah then attempts to interpret R. Eliezer differently, but his suggestion is dismissed by Abbaye. R. Ashi then attempts another reinterpretation of R. Eliezer, but the Tosafists have pointed out that this is counter to the accepted halakha (see R. Samuel Edel's comments in *Maharsha*).
    Cf. Chapter Six.

15. This is manifest from many passages in the Talmud. See Ze'ev Jawitz, *Toledot Israel*, 6:35; *Otzar Israel, Encyclopedia Judaica, et al.*

16. One Talmudic passage (Gittin 56A) refers to the Zealots as *Beryoni;* another (Avot D'Rabbi Nathan 6:3) calls them *Kanna'im*, the actual title used by the group, while the Mishnah also employs the term *Sikarim* (Sicarii; Machshirin 1:6). Students of Josephus are well acquainted with the historian's reluctance to refer to them as *Kanna'im*, probably because the term had previously been a title of distinction among the priests (*kohanim*).

17. R. Eliezer is also the author of the statement (Bava Mezia 59B) that a proselyte "has a strong inclination to evil."

18. The Talmud (Gittin 56A) specifically blamed the destruction on R. Zechariah ben Avkulot, a sage-priest who refused to accept a sacrifice containing a minor blemish from the Emperor, even though the Rabbis had permitted it. Josephus also records that the war was caused by the Jews' refusal to accept the Emperor's sacrifice in 66 C.E. (Wars 2:17, 409–410). Scholars such as Derenbourg and Eisenstein have identified him as the Zealot leader and priest Zacharias son of Amphicalleus mentioned by Josephus (Wars 4:225). (K. Kohler [*Jewish Encyclopedia* 12:642] errs by listing him as a Shammaite on the basis of the Tosefta [Shabbat 17:6], for the Tosefta there states explicitly that he followed neither School with regard to a ruling concerning the Sabbath.)

19. The Talmud states that thirty of Hillel's disciples were worthy of the Divine Spirit resting upon them, as it did upon Moses— a reference to prophecy. (See Sanhedrin 11A and Rashi *ad loc*.

regarding Samuel the Little.) Another thirty of Hillel's disciples are described as having been worthy that the sun should stand still for them, as it did for Joshua the son of Nun, which might also be a reference to prophecy.

20. See 1 Kings (19:10, 14) where the Prophet Elijah accuses the Jewish people of his time of slaying God's prophets. Is it possible that the prophets amongst the Hasidim were targets of persecution for many centuries prior to Jesus' time? If so, it is highly possible that the Zechariah ben Berechiah referred to by Jesus in Matthew 23 lived hundreds of years earlier.

21. Wellhausen's interpretation may be found in the *Loeb Classical Library*, Josephus, note to Wars 4:334–344.

22. Talmudic evidence clearly indicates that it was at about the time of Jesus that the title "rabbi" began to be used. R. Jehiel Heilprin (*Seder Hadorot*, p. 151) maintains that Simeon, son of Hillel, was the first to use the title, while others have suggested R. Gamaliel the Elder, Hillel's grandson. Some find it difficult to accept that Hillel's family, famed for their humility, should have been the scholars to initiate this practice. I believe it highly possible then that Jesus is telling us that Bet Shammai were the first to be known as Rabbi.

23. Another example might be Jesus' reference to the Pharisees as "vipers," which is analogous to the criticism of the Pharisees in the Damascus Document of the Essenes, based on Isaiah (59:5), "their webs are spiders' webs and their eggs basilisks' eggs." I have demonstrated in Chapter Six, note 12, that this criticism is related to the debate between Bet Shammai and Bet Hillel over the levirate marriage issue of "the daughter's rival" (*Tzarat Ha-Bat*, Yevamot 2A–16A), in which Bet Hillel considered Bet Shammai's children to be bastards.

Yet another valid example is Jesus' teaching and association with sinners (Matthew 9:10 *et al.*). This appears related to another debate where Bet Shammai held that the Torah should be taught only to one who is wise, humble, of good family and rich, whereas Bet Hillel ruled that one should teach to all (Avot D'Rabbi Nathan, end ch. 2).

24. As for our earlier quote from Luke 2, where Jesus as a young-ster was found among the Doctors of the Law in the Temple, we can only speculate as to their identity. It would seem that they were leading scholars, not known as "Pharisees," and that he cherished this memory later in life. If they were Shammai and his disciples, he would have surely regretted the incident, given their view of the Gentile world. His age is given as twelve at the time, which would have been 10 C.E., the year of Hillel's death (according to A. Hyman, *Toledot Tanna'im*). There is a good chance therefore that they were Hillel and his few disci-ples, which meeting might have had a strong effect on his fu-ture.

25. The Jerusalem Talmud (Yoma 6:3) states that these doors were locked each night, but would be found open in the morning.

26. The lot (upon which was written "for the Lord") placed by the High Priest on the sin-offering of Yom Kippur did not come up any longer in his right hand; nor did the crimson-dyed strap turn white (upon the sending of the he-goat on Yom Kippur, a sign in earlier times that their sins had been forgiven); nor did the western-most light (of the Menorah) shine.

27. I have discussed this little-known passage of the Tosefta with several scholars, and it has evoked surprise, since it is com-monly assumed that the "hatred without cause" existed among the Jews themselves. If we insist on maintaining the latter stance, the Tosefta would be telling us that when brotherhood is finally achieved with the Gentiles, hatred will disappear amongst Jews as well.

It is also difficult to understand the Tosefta's quotation from the second verse (Jeremiah 31) regarding the "watch-men," since many such prophecies abound in Scripture. How-ever, the text's Hebrew term for "watchmen" is *Notzrim,* which is also Hebrew for Christians (the Tosefta first appeared in the third century); the Tosefta may thus be telling us that in the era of the future Temple—when the "hatred" will no longer exist—the *"notzrim,"* or Christians, will be welcomed.

The author of this passage in the Tosefta is R. Johanan

ben Torta, a Sage who had converted to Judaism in the early second century C.E. He is quoted in the Jerusalem Talmud (Ta'anit 4:8) as telling R. Akiva—who believed Bar Kokhba to be the Messiah, as he waged war against the Romans in 135 C.E.—"Akiva! Grass shall grow from your jaws before the son of David appears." I have been unable to find a single commentary attempting to explain why R. Johanan was so certain that Bar Kokhba wasn't the Messiah. However, in light of his statement in the Tosefta, it is possible that he was alluding to the fact that Bar Kokhba's rebellion was only a war of liberation, lacking any movement to bring Gentiles a message of salvation.

Finally, with regard to Jesus' mission of bringing the Gentiles closer to the Torah of Moses through observance of the Noahide Laws, I have previously noted that according to the Talmud (Sanhedrin 57A) and Maimonides (*Melakhim*, ch. 8), Moses obligated the Jews to spread knowledge of the Noahide Commandments to the Gentiles only from a position of strength, and since they never attained such power the obligation never went into effect. Such a mission to the Gentiles would have therefore been beyond the letter of the law (*lifnim mishurat hadin*). The Talmud (Bava Mezia 30B) gives the reason for Jerusalem's destruction as the people's unwillingness to act beyond the letter of the law, and it may well be that it was just such a mission the Talmud had in mind. This would serve as a reply to the query raised by the Tosafists (*ibid.*) from Yoma 9B, where the reason is given as Hatred Without Cause. According to my interpretation, both Talmudic passages are really one and the same—namely, the Jews' relationship with the Gentiles.

28. It would be difficult to summarily blame the Jews for their hatred of the Gentiles, since they had suffered so much from them even in those days. "Without cause" would therefore have to be understood as the Jews' obligation to see the potential of the Gentile world once they have been brought closer to the Torah of Moses. Perhaps this is the meaning of the previously

quoted Talmudic passage citing the Jews' unwillingness to go beyond the Letter of the Law as the reason for Jerusalem's destruction (see end of note 27).

29. See Joseph Klausner, *Jesus of Nazareth,* pp. 343 and 348.

   (Cf. Chapter Three, note 19, where I noted that Essene-Pharisees of the first century—such as "Abba" Saul—were known [Niddah 25B] as Son of Man [*Bar Nash*]. It is significant that Jesus identified himself as "son of man" at his trial.)

30 The Hebrew term used in the Midrash is "*tzibbur.*"

31. This interpretation is offered by R. Moses Margoliot (*Penei Moshe*) and the Gaon of Vilna in their eighteenth century commentaries to the Jerusalem Talmud, as well as by many Halakhists.

32. Such Halakhists as Maimonides (*Yesodei Ha-Torah* 5:5) and R. David ben Samuel Halevy (*Turei Zahav, Shulhan Arukh Yoreh Deah* 157:7) have struggled with Eliahu Ha-Navi's censure of the sage, since the latter had obviously acted in accordance with the law.

33. Thus, the one identified by the Gentiles comes under the ruling of "*rodef*" or pursuer of an innocent person.

   The Tosefta's ruling is derived from the biblical account concerning Sheva ben Bichri, who was handed over to Joab (2 Samuel 20). See Rashi (Sanhedrin 72B) for the Halakhic considerations involved in Sheva ben Bichri's case.

34. The term *Brit Hadasha* (new covenant) appears in Jeremiah (31:30), as well as in the Damascus Document found at Qumran. We have previously identified this Scroll as having been written by the disciples of Menahem and Hillel, who joined the Essenes in order to establish a religion for the Gentiles.

35. The Gospels identify Judas Iscariot as the one who betrayed Jesus. Scholars have suggested that the puzzling epithet "Iscariot" is derived from *Sicarii*, the term used to describe the Zealots (see *Encyclopedia Judaica* 14:1492). We have previously established that these murderers followed the teachings of Bet Shammai, and we may thus understand why he opposed Jesus. Luke (22:3) links Judas with the devil, and we have

earlier noted the Talmud's linking of Bet Shammai with Satan (see note 13).

36. R. Joshua ben Levi is quoted in the Talmud (Rosh Ha-Shanah 19B) as giving testimony concerning the Jewish calendar according to the *Kehilla Kaddisha D'Yerushalayim* (Holy Community of Jerusalem, also known as the *Edah Kedoshah* or Holy Congregation)—a group founded by second century disciples of R. Meir—which scholars have identified as having contained remnants of the Essene brotherhood (see Soncino, editor, *ibid.* and *Jewish Encyclopedia* 5:226). We thus find a direct relationship between R. Joshua and the Essene Hasidim.

(I have previously noted in this book that although the term "Hasid" is used at times in the Talmud to describe any pious person, it also unquestionably alludes to a particular group, such as Hillel and his disciples [Sanhedrin 11A] and the Essenes ["Scroll of the Hasidim," Jerusalem Talmud, end Berakhot, and "Cave of the Hasidim," Mo'ed Katan 17A]. See also Kiddushin 71A, where [according to R. Samuel Edels, *Maharsha, Aggadot,* sixth note] the Talmud equates the attitude of the Essenes with that of the prophet Elijah with regard to not speaking aught that might prove detrimental to others. Cf. Avodah Zarah 20B where a Baraita lists Hasidism as superior to Pharisaism in the listing of degrees leading to spiritual perfection.)

37. See Talmud (Yevamot 36A) where it is ruled that R. Johanan's position is always accepted over that of Resh Lakish, with three specific exceptions (the dispute cited here is not among the three). This question was first raised on Maimonides in R. Meir Ha-Kohen of Rothenberg's thirteenth century work *Haggahot Maimuniyyot,* who offers no reply. Cf. R. Moses Margoliot's commentary *Mareh Ha-Panim* to the Jerusalem Talmud where he concludes that no plausible solution can be offered to explain Maimonides' adoption of Resh Lakish's view. Our interpretation of this passage in the Jerusalem Talmud—linking it with Jesus' crucifixion—thus offers a satisfactory reply to the difficult question raised on Maimonides, as Resh Lakish's opin-

ion represents the true "Mishnah of the Hasidim" (Bet Hillel) in this case.

38. The Babylonian Talmud (Yevamot 15B) gives the family name as Kuppai, while the Jerusalem Talmud (Yevamot 1:6) mentions Nekifi.

The term would apply to Caiaphas' acceptance of the Shammaite-Zealot view, or to his interpretation of the law.

8.

UNDERSTANDING THE CHRISTIAN BIBLE THROUGH BET SHAMMAI AND BET HILLEL

Theologians have generally assumed, primarily on the basis of specific references by Jesus to Jewish law contained in the Gospels, that the founder of Christianity was antitraditionalist. Rabbi Emden's thesis demands that these references be reexamined. This chapter allows for a limited analysis of several such passages.

Rabbi Emden asserts in his letter that Jesus allowed his disciples to desecrate the Sabbath (Matthew 12), so that the Gentile followers of his new faith should not observe the weekly day of rest in the Jewish manner, which would be a violation of the Noahide Code (see Sanhedrin 58B). It may be noted that when the Pharisees complained to Jesus about his disciples' desecration of the Sabbath, he first quoted from Hosea (6:6), where the Prophet represents God as desiring mercy (*hesed*), then refers to his disciples as "innocent," and then concludes: "The son of man is master of the Sabbath." I would suggest that since the alleged work was not intended for its usual purpose, but rather for an ulterior result, it would be classified as "a labor not required on its own account" (see Shabbat 73B *et al.*), for which there is no liability. A similar thesis is advanced by the sixteenth century Talmudist R. Samuel Edels in a parallel case involving a biblical personality (*Maharsha*, Bava Batra 119A, Aggadot). The

Tosafists (Betsah 8A, second paragraph) have pointed out that such labor would be completely permissible if necessary for a constructive religious purpose, even according to Bet Shammai (see *Maharsha ad loc.*). However, the Pharisees of Bet Shammai would certainly not have agreed with Jesus' concept of mercy (*hesed*) here, as they opposed his mission to the Gentiles.

The Gospel (Matthew 12:9–14) then relates that Jesus healed a man on the Sabbath, and was criticized by the Pharisees for doing so. Since Jesus evidently healed through prayer, this incident appears to refer to a dispute between Bet Shammai and Bet Hillel over whether it is permitted to pray for the sick on the Sabbath (Tosefta Shabbat 17:14); Bet Hillel permitted such prayer, and Bet Shammai forbade it. In the Gospel according to Mark (2:27), Jesus concludes his argument with the Pharisees concerning the Sabbath by stating, "The Sabbath was made for man, not man for the Sabbath." In addition to prayer for the sick, this would allude to other disputes between the two schools, such as where Bet Shammai rule that it is forbidden on the Sabbath to promise charity for the poor in the synagogue, even for the marriage of orphans, nor may betrothals be arranged, nor may discussion be held for a youngster's education, nor may mourners be comforted or the sick visited, while Bet Hillel permit all of these (Tosefta Shabbat 17:14 and Shabbat 12A). Other examples could be cited.

The Gospel according to Matthew (ch. 15) has the Pharisees complaining to Jesus that his disciples do not wash their hands before eating. Luke (11:37) relates that a Pharisee invited Jesus for a meal, and was surprised that Jesus didn't wash his hands first. Jesus replied, "Now you Pharisees cleanse the outside of the cup . . ." and this leads into an attack on the Pharisees similar to Matthew 23. Washing hands before meals has its source in the eighteen measures (Shabbat

13B–15A), and would have no relationship to Jesus' remark concerning the "outside of the cup." Jesus is clearly referring here to the dispute between the two Schools over when the washing should take place (Mishnah, Berakhot 51B). According to the Talmud (*ibid.* 43A), meals of the Pharisees would begin with the drinking of a cup of wine, after which they would break bread together. Bet Shammai held that the hands must be washed before filling the cup of wine, whereas Bet Hillel ruled that the washing should take place later, before partaking of the bread. The Talmud (*ibid.*, 52A–B) explains that Bet Shammai were concerned that the cup of wine might become ritually unclean from the hands, whereas Bet Hillel held that it is permitted to use a cup which had become unclean from the outside. The passage in Luke is therefore telling us that Jesus upheld Bet Hillel's ruling concerning the outside of the cup, and wished to wash later, before the bread. The Talmud further makes clear that Bet Shammai considered those following Bet Hillel's ruling as eating with unclean hands (as the unclean cup could defile the hands), and this explains the accusation against the disciples.[1]

Matthew 15 has Jesus rebuking the Pharisees for permitting one to consecrate all his possessions to the Temple, which would lead to family poverty, and I have demonstrated in Chapter Six that this was the Talmudic stance of R. Eliezer the Shammaite (Shabbat 127B). This would have been further exacerbated by Bet Shammai's position (Nazir 9A) that one could never be released from a vow made to the Temple.

Jesus further identifies his adversaries (Matthew 23:23; Luke 11:42) as "you pay tithe of mint and anise and cummin." This is an obvious reference to R. Eliezer's stringent rulings (Ma'asrot 4:5,6) regarding such plants and trees grown for their seed, the Sage holding that not only the seed, but also the leaves, pods and stalks were to be tithed as well. Once again Jesus identifies the Shammaites as the target of his criticism, their opinion on this matter recorded in the Mishnah under the name of R. Eliezer the Shammaite.

R. Emden also believes in his letter that Christian baptism was modeled after the ritual immersion of converts to Judaism. Here, too, we find a divergence between the Schools over the importance attached to ritual ablution upon entering the faith. According to the Talmud (Yevamot 46B), R. Joshua of Bet Hillel held that both males and females performed such ablution when the Israelites received the Torah at Mount Sinai, whereas R. Eliezer the Shammaite believed that men underwent circumcision only, and he makes no mention of any ceremony for women.

Jesus Attacks the Moneychangers at the Temple

Jesus (Matthew 23:16–21) states that his Pharisee antagonists viewed a vow by the Temple or Altar as not binding, and he disagrees (i.e., if one declares "this item shall be forbidden to me just as pleasure from the Temple or Altar are forbidden to me." The halakhic principle involved here is that the vow must refer to things which are forbidden because of a vow, such as sacrifices. Since the Altar and Temple are forbidden by the Torah itself, does the vower actually intend the Temple and Altar, or the sacrifices which are brought to them?). Since Jesus' view here corresponds with that of the Mishnah (Nedarim 10B; i.e., that the vower's intent is the sacrifices brought through a vow), we may ask: Who are these dissenting Pharisees? There also appears to be no relationship between this argument and his preceding criticism of these Pharisees' view of the Gentiles.

I would suggest that Jesus is criticizing an early Shammaite view adhered to by the Zealot priests (the Zealots' power-base and leadership seem to have always been centered in the priesthood. Such leaders as Zadok the Pharisee, Eleazar ben Hananiah and Zechariah ben Avkulot were all priests), which would have enabled them to refuse many offerings of Gentiles to the Temple. We know from Josephus that by the year 66 C.E. the Zealots refused all gifts of Gentiles to the Temple, and they were surely inclined to some such behavior in Jesus' time. According to the Mishnah (Shekalim 1:5), only sacrifices which could be vowed or brought as free-will offerings were accepted from Gentiles, whereas it was at the option of the priests to accept gifts for Temple repairs or upkeep from non-Jews (Arakhin 6A; Maimonides, *Matnot Aniyim* 8:8). Most offerings from Gentiles were surely given for "the Temple" or "the Altar"—we should assume they were unfamiliar with the intricacies of these laws—and the Shammaite Pharisees' ruling on vows would have enabled the Zealot priests to refuse such gifts, or even pocket the money themselves—since they were not specifically earmarked for sacrifices, and formulas such as "the Temple" or "the Altar" were not to be interpreted as referring to sacrifices. (That many gifts were offered by Gentiles is evident from Josephus, Wars 5:17, who records ". . . that altar universally venerated by Greeks and barbarians.")

This could explain Jesus' attack on the moneychangers at the Temple (Matthew 21:12–13; Mark 11:15–17), for it was their function to accept all gifts and forward them to their intended purpose (Shekalim 6:5,6). It was at these moneychangers' tables that the Zealot priests would have diverted the Gentile offerings. This is well-documented in Jesus' charge at the time that instead of the Temple being a "house of prayer for all nations" (Isaiah 56:7), it had instead become a "den of thieves" (Jeremiah 7:11). (I have previously noted that the Talmud and Josephus referred to the Zealots as murderers and thieves. Cf. Damascus Document, 6:15, where the authors resolve not to defile themselves by laying hands "on that which has been vowed or devoted to God or on the property of the Temple.")

The Mishnah would have later omitted this early Shammaite view, since they apparently abandoned it. I have previously demonstrated that R. Eliezer later reversed the early Shammaite stance—also criticized by Jesus—permitting one to vow all his possessions to the Temple. It is also apparent from the Talmud (Gittin 56A) that Bet Shammai eventually broke away—at least partially—from the Zealots, as R. Eliezer helped R. Johanan ben Zakkai leave Jerusalem to negotiate with Vespasian, despite the Zealots' objections and threats.

Jesus (in Matthew 23) is then actually criticizing the reluctance of the Shammaites and Zealots to accept sacrifices from the Gentiles, a practice which eventually led (through refusal of the Emperor's sacrifice) to the Temple's destruction.

Returning once again to the Sabbath issue, we find Jesus healing a paralyzed man on the Sabbath, and telling him to carry his bed away with him (John 5). The Pharisees considered this a violation of the Sabbath. It is usually assumed that Jesus permitted the man to carry, as Jesus was a violator of the Sabbath law. But Jerusalem was a walled city, and there would have been no reason to forbid such carrying. I believe rather that the Shammaite Pharisees considered the bed to have become *mukzah* (an object one does not intend to use during the Sabbath) after the healing, and therefore forbidden to be moved. Jesus, however, adopted Rava's view (Betsah 26B; *Shulhan Arukh Orah Haim* 310:3) holding that the prohibition of *mukzah* does not apply where the state developed after the beginning of the Sabbath. The fourth century Rava was well-known as a hasid (see Chapter Three), so once again we find

Jesus adhering to the authentic traditions of the Hasidim. The Talmud (Betsah 26B) does in fact record a conflicting view which forbade moving such an object on the Sabbath.

Jesus gives various rulings on divorce in the Gospels, and this book will not attempt to meddle in the various interpretations accepted by different Christian denominations. However, it might be pointed out that the Jerusalem Talmud (Kiddushin 1:1) establishes a very basic difference between divorce among Jews and Gentiles. A Jewish husband divorces his wife by giving her a written bill of divorcement (usually termed a "*get*"), in accordance with Deuteronomy 24:1. However, the Jerusalem Talmud infers from a verse in Malachi (2:16) that this does not apply to Gentiles under the Noahide system. This led to a difference of opinion among the Talmudic sages.[2] Some held that no divorce is possible among Gentiles, while others believed that divorce among Gentiles can be effected by either husband or wife leaving the other spouse, without need of a written document.[3]

It would seem that Jesus (Matthew 5:31–32) did not wish his followers to practice the rules of written divorce outlined in Deuteronomy, which would support this book's central thesis that Jesus wished to establish a religion for the Gentiles based on the Noahide system. Jesus (Matthew 19:5–6) further bases his teachings concerning divorce on a verse in Genesis (2:24), and this verse is expressly discussed in the Talmud (Sanhedrin 58A) as applying to the Noahide Laws.[4]

BOTH ARE THE WORDS OF THE LIVING GOD

I should note here that I have been deeply troubled by the apparently negative picture this book projects of the School of Shammai. After all, hadn't the Heavenly Voice stated explicitly that "both are the words of the Living God"?

And doesn't the Talmud state expressly (Yevamot 14B) that "love and friendship" existed between the two Schools?

A careful analysis would however indicate that the relationship of the two Schools with one another was not uniform throughout their existence. Their initial debates portray a degree of suspicion and hostility (see Chapters Three and Seven); the love and friendship is evidenced mainly in the later times of R. Eliezer and R. Joshua. Also germane to such an analysis are the Mishnahs (Eduyyot 1:7, 8, 10, 11) where the School of Shammai disputes Shammai, thus proving that Shammai the Elder lost some measure of control over his school; no such halakhic disputes ever developed between Hillel and his disciples. The Talmud (Eruvin 13B) further intimates that Bet Shammai did not entertain the opinions of Bet Hillel seriously, which would have had a most deleterious effect on their scholarship.

The most rational approach appears to be that Bet Shammai were entirely sincere in their effort to secure and improve the lot of their people. Nor is there any evidence that they actually supported the violence of the Zealots against the innocent. (See Kiddushin 43A where Shammai the Elder rules that one who sends a second party to commit a murder is himself liable for the crime. Could he have issued this solitary opinion as a warning to Bet Shammai that they would be held accountable for the Zealots' crimes?) This surely entitles their opinions to be remembered as "the words of the Living God."

It would in fact be more plausible and simpler to suggest that Bet Shammai's opinions came to be considered "the words of the living God" during the latter part of the first century C.E., and not during the earlier period of their existence. During that later time they indeed showed love and friendship toward Bet Hillel, and they also apparently severed their ties with the Zealots. This is evidenced by R. Eliezer assisting R. Johanan ben Zakkai to leave Jerusalem in order to negotiate with the Romans, despite the Zealots' opposition to such talks (Gittin 56A). I have also previously noted (Chapter Seven, note 18) that R. Zechariah ben Avkulot, a leading Zealot priest-Pharisee during the late first century C.E., followed neither Bet Hillel nor Bet Shammai with regard to a point of Jewish law—thus indicating that the Zealots were no longer joined to Bet Shammai.

THE SCRIBES AND THE HASIDIM

This book has concentrated primarily on the era of the two Schools, and not on the previous periods dating back to the time of the Maccabees (c. 165 B.C.E.) or earlier. See 1 Maccabees 7:12, 13 where the Scribes (*Soferim*) and the Hasidim are presented as two separate and distinct groups. Ample evidence exists to demonstrate that both the Scribes and the Hasidim had their origins as far back as the time of Moses, while the term "Pharisee" first appears shortly before the Common Era. It was apparently not before the first century B.C.E. that the hostility between these groups surfaced. It was at the turn of this era that "the Torah became as two Torahs" (Sanhedrin 88B). And it was during this crucial period that Bet Shammai came to dominate the "Scribes and Pharisees."

See Chapter Three where I presented Talmudic evidence (Berakhot 6B and Sanhedrin 11A) that no sage living amongst the general populace during the Talmudic era was known openly as a Hasid during his lifetime, including those of Bet Hillel. We thus find R. Gamaliel, grandson of Hillel, referred to as a Pharisee in the Acts of the Apostles (5:34). It also seems fairly obvious that the Pharisees who warned Jesus that his life was in danger (Luke 13:31) were of the Hasidim. The secretive background of the Essene Hasidim would explain why no mention of them appears in the Gospels.

With regard to Bet Hillel's links with the Essenes, the following additional points may be noted.

It is evident from the Talmudic narrative concerning Samuel the Little (Berakhot 28B) that R. Gamaliel's benediction against the Jewish-Christians was initially recited once annually. The Manual of Discipline (1:18–3:12) records that the Essene Hasidim convened once annually to renew their covenant, at which time their leaders pronounced similar statements against those of "Belial's lot" and strayers. Could this have been the same yearly event?

The Damascus Document (14:3) casually mentions the presence of proselytes within their camp. Considering Bet Shammai's harsh attitude toward converts, it would have been only natural for them to gravitate toward the Essene-Hillelite Hasidim, who regarded them as equals.

The Mishnah (Betsah 21B) informs us that Hillel's family observed certain stringent rulings of Bet Shammai, even though the community at large was not required to do so. Bet Shammai imposed their difficult ways upon all the people, and this is apparently the intent of Jesus' criticism (Matthew 23:4). It would appear then that the halakhas of the Dead Sea Scrolls cannot be studied on a comparative basis, as this dual system implies that many of the Hasidim's rigid rulings were meant for themselves only.

CONCLUSION

This chapter—as the others preceding it—is based on the writings of Rabbi Jacob Emden, the great eighteenth century Talmudist and mystic. My contribution to his thesis has consisted in the main of connecting what Jesus of Nazareth apparently perceived as his mission with the positions of the two leading Schools of Rabbis in the first century, as well as to analyze the similarities between the Dead Sea Scrolls of the Essene Hasidim and the Christian Bible.

The most relevant lessons which we of the twentieth century may derive from this analysis would be connected to the ideals of brotherly love and peace, which are the goals of modern society.

Jesus of Nazareth—according to our thesis—never wished to see his fellow Jews change one iota of their traditional faith. He himself remained an Orthodox Jew to his last moment. He only wished to see his people return to the teachings of the School of Hillel, which stressed love, humility, and the salvation of all mankind. His attacks on the Pharisees were directed against the School of Shammai, who were in control of the principal institutions of Judaism in his time. Accordingly, there seems no question that the Hasid from Nazareth would have objected strenuously to Christian missionary activity among Jews.

Another important conclusion is that the Jewish people of today do not identify with the "Scribes and Pharisees" whom he condemned. To the contrary, the Talmud states explicitly that a Jew who follows the teachings of Bet Shammai "deserves death." Hence, there is no basis for Christian enmity toward the Jews of today because of the actions of certain individuals who lived in the first century. We do not identify with them nor with their teachings. A Heavenly Voice settled the matter toward the close of the first century: "The Halakha is as Bet Hillel."

It is my fervent hope that these writings will make a contribution toward bringing all men and women who seek God and the brotherhood of humanity into a closer bond of fellowship. If we achieve this, we may hope to merit being considered among the disciples of the prophet Elijah, who, according to the Mishnah (Eduyyot 8:7), will appear before the coming of the Messiah to bring peace to mankind.

For as Rabbi Jacob Emden[5] wrote (*Seder Olam* 34A): "In the name of Heaven, we are your brothers; one God has created us all."[6]

NOTES

1. It is manifest from these passages in the Gospels that the washing of hands before everyday meals was widely practiced among the people in Jesus' time. This custom had its origin in one of the "eighteen measures" passed by Bet Shammai, requiring that *Terumah* (the priest's share of the produce) not be eaten by the priests without first washing the hands (Shabbat 13B). This washing was later extended to everyday meals eaten by all Jews (Hullin 106A). The Gospels thus provide clear proof that the debate between the two Schools over the eighteen measures took place before 30 C.E., the time of Jesus' preaching.

   The exact dating of the debate over the eighteen measures has become enmeshed in scholarly controversy. If the debate indeed took place before Jesus' time—as is evident from the Gospels—it would help explain the hostile attitude of Jesus toward the Pharisees, as members of Bet Hillel were killed by Bet Shammai during the debate (our position has been that Zealots were responsible for the killings). We have also pointed out in earlier chapters that following this debate, Hillel's surviving disciples left to join the Essenes in establishing a religion for the Gentiles.

   The Tosafists (Shabbat 14B) have pointed out that Hillel and Shammai were both present at the debate (on the basis of Shabbat 17A and Tosefta Shabbat 1:8), which would date the event before 10 C.E., the year of Hillel's passing. Dr. Sid Leiman (*The Canonization of Hebrew Scripture*, 1976) quotes the eminent Talmudist R. Zevi Hirsch Chajes (*Kol Sifrei Maharaz Chajes* 1:153) as fixing the date between 30 to 10 B.C.E. on the basis of further Talmudic evidence. Zacharias Frankel (*Darkei HaMishnah*), a leading historian of the period, has also listed the event as taking place during the beginning of the two Schools' existence, or prior to the Common Era.

It would seem then that individual theories attempting to place the debate at a later date in the first century C.E.—such as those advanced by H. Graetz (c. 66 C.E.) and Isaac H. Weiss (c. 44 C.E.)—should not be heeded, as they only serve to confuse the student of history.

2. See R. Moses Margoliot's explanatory notes in his *Penei Moshe*.
3. This halakhic controversy over divorce among Gentiles continued into the Middle Ages. The fourteenth century Spanish Talmudist R. Nissim ben Reuben Gerondi (*Hiddushei HaRan*, Sanhedrin 58B) cites authoritative opinion contending that no divorce is possible among Gentiles, while Maimonides (*Melakhim* 9:8) adopted the view that divorce can be brought about by either spouse leaving the other.

Some have tried to relate Jesus' views on divorce with a three-way dispute on the subject between Bet Shammai, Bet Hillel and R. Akiva (Mishnah, Gittin 90A). But the discussion there centers on Jewish divorce, and all three support their stances by quoting from Deuteronomy 24:1 which deals with the Jewish Bill of Divorcement. It should further be noted that all three agreed to divorce where both husband and wife consented; they only disagreed as to under what conditions the husband could divorce his wife against her will (divorce against the wife's will was permitted in Judaism until the tenth century C.E.).

4. Dr. Joseph Sievers, a Catholic scholar, has drawn my attention to the belief of some scholars that the authors of the Dead Sea Scrolls prohibited divorce, and that Jesus may have concurred with them. A thorough study of the Scrolls does not justify such a stance.

The term for divorce (*la-megaresh*) appears once in the Damascus Document (13:17), and C. Rabin has reconstructed this incomplete sentence to show that the Qumranites practiced divorce (see Y. Yadin's introduction to the Temple Scroll, p. 273). At the time the Damascus Document was first discovered in the Cairo Genizah, Solomon Schechter indeed attempted to interpret one passage as not recognizing divorce, but Louis Ginzberg dismissed his suggestion (*An Unknown Jewish Sect*, p. 20). Some have also tried to infer from a passage in the Temple Scroll (p. 57) that a Jewish king was prohibited to divorce his wife, but precedent for this may be found in the Talmud (Sanhedrin 22A) where it is related that King David was not permitted to divorce any of his wives. The important point here is that such a prohibition would have applied to a king only, and not to the rest of the people. The Jerusalem Talmud (Sanhedrin 2:3) in fact does discuss the status of a woman divorced by the king.

Judaism of course discourages divorce, but has always recognized its validity. The royal Davidic line was established through David's marriage to Bathsheba—she having been Solomon's mother—and she had been divorced by Uriah the Hittite. This is based on the rabbinic tradition that all soldiers leaving to David's wars divorced their wives first (see Ketubbot 9B).

5. While writing this book, I have often drawn inspiration from the fact that my family traces its lineage to R. Jacob Joshua Falk (1680–1756)—author of the famed Talmudic Novellae *Penei Ye-hoshua*—who was R. Emden's staunchest supporter as he waged battle against the Shabbateans. May their memories bring a blessing.

6. His plea is derived from a Talmudic passage (Rosh Ha-Shanah 19A), which also appears in the Megillat Ta'anit.

A BIOGRAPHICAL LISTING
OF JEWISH SAGES AND SCHOLARS
REFERRED TO IN THIS BOOK

Sages of the Mishnah
Early and Later Tanna'im
Second Century B.C.E. to Second Century C.E.

ABBA SAUL (first-second centuries C.E.) Scholars have expressed the view that two sages by this name lived during the period.

AKIVA (first century C.E. – 135 C.E.) One of the most important figures in the period of the Mishnah. Died as a martyr.

BAVA BEN BUTA (first century B.C.E.) Although a member of Bet Shammai, he supported Bet Hillel in an early dispute between the Schools over sacrifice on the Festivals.

DOSA BEN HARKINAS (first-second century C.E.) Criticized his brother Jonathan for supporting Bet Shammai in a case involving levirate marriage.

ELEAZAR BEN ARAKH (second half of the first century C.E.) An outstanding disciple of R. Johanan ben Zakkai.

ELEAZAR BEN HANANIAH (first century C.E.) A leader of Bet Shammai, son of Hananiah ben Hezekiah.

162

ELIEZER BEN HYRCANUS (first and second centuries C.E.) A leading sage of Bet Shammai, who never deviated from their teachings. He held salvation of the Gentiles to be impossible. Was eventually excommunicated by the rabbis.

GAMALIEL THE ELDER (first half of first century C.E.) Grandson of Hillel, Nasi (pres.) of the Sanhedrin, teacher of Paul the Apostle, intervened to save the lives of early Christian apostles.

GAMALIEL OF YAVNEH (second half of first century C.E.) Descendant of Hillel, Nasi (pres.) of the Sanhedrin at Yavneh.

HANANIAH BEN HEZEKIAH (first century B.C.E.) Sage in whose house Bet Shammai decreed the Eighteen Measures, which were designed to create greater separation from the Gentiles.

HILLEL (end of first century B.C.E. and beginning of first century C.E.) Nasi (pres.) of the Sanhedrin from 30 B.C.E. to 10 C.E., founder of Bet Hillel; he is especially remembered for his teachings concerning love for one's fellow-man, his humility and his warm relations with both Jews and Gentiles.

HIYYA (end of second century C.E.) Tanna and Amora, pupil and associate of Judah Ha-Nasi, teacher of Rav.

ISSI BEN JUDAH (second century C.E.) Tanna, he is identified in Talmudic sources with other names.

JOHANAN BEN TORTA (first half of second century C.E.) A convert to Judaism.

JOHANAN BEN ZAKKAI (first century C.E.) Member of Bet Hillel, Nasi of the Sanhedrin at the time of the Second Temple's destruction in 70 C.E., headed the Sanhedrin at Yavneh afterwards.

JONATHAN BEN HARKINAS (late first century C.E.) Leader of Bet Shammai.

JOSE BEN JOEZER (first half of second century B.C.E.) Served as Nasi of the Sanhedrin.

JOSHUA (BEN HANANIAH) (first and second centuries C.E.) Member of Bet Hillel, a leading sage toward close of first century, recorded Bet Hillel's position that righteous Gentiles merit salvation.

JOSHUA BEN PERACHIAH (second half of second century B.C.E. and early first century B.C.E.) Nasi of the Sanhedrin, teacher of a Yeshua Ha-Notzri who has been confused with the Founder of Christianity.

JUDAH BEN BAVA (second century C.E.) Tanna and martyr.

JUDAH HA-NASI (latter half of the second century and beginning of third century C.E.) Descendant of Hillel, redactor of the Mishnah.

MEIR (second century C.E.) Spiritual father of the Kehilla Kaddisha De-Yerushalayim, which scholars have identified as having contained remnants of the Essene community; taught that a Gentile who studies the Noahide commandments is considered the equal of a high priest.

MENAHEM THE ESSENE (first century B.C.E.) Served as Av Bet Din (v.p.) of the Sanhedrin under Hillel, left with 160 scholars on a mission to the Gentiles when Shammai replaced him.

PHINEAS BEN JAIR (second half of second century C.E.) Author of Baraita listing degrees leading to spiritual perfection.

SAMUEL THE LITTLE (early first century C.E.) Member of Bet Hillel, composed the benediction against the Minim (Jewish-Christians) at the request of R. Gamaliel the Elder.

SHAMMAI (c. 50 B.C.E. – c. 30 C.E.) Av Bet Din (v.p.) of the Sandhedrin, founder of the School of Shammai; he is described by the Talmud as an impatient man, especially in his relations with Gentiles.

SIMEON (early first century C.E.) Son of Hillel, served as Nasi (pres.) of the Sanhedrin.

SIMEON BEN GAMALIEL (first century C.E.) Great-grandson of Hillel, Nasi (pres.) of the Sanhedrin, died as a martyr.

TARFON (late first century C.E.) Tanna at Yavneh, ruled in accordance with Bet Shammai on several matters and was criticized by the rabbis.

ZADOK (late first century B.C.E. and early first century C.E.) Member of Bet Shammai who later joined Bet Hillel; according to Josephus, he was a founder of the Zealots.

ZECHARIA BEN AVKULOT (first century C.E.) The Talmud blamed him for the destruction of the Temple, as he had refused the Roman Emperor's sacrifice. Modern scholars have identified him as a Zealot.

Sages of the Talmud
The Amoraim
Third to Fifth Centuries C.E.

ABBAYE (278–338 C.E.) Headed the Yeshiva in Pumbedita, colleague of Rava.

ASHI (c. 335–427/28 C.E.) Headed the Yeshiva at Sura.

ASSI (early third century C.E.) A contemporary of Rav and Samuel, lived in Babylonia.

HUNA (second half of third century) Headed the Yeshiva at Sura.

JOHANAN (c. 180–c. 279) Palestinian Amora, quoted often in both the Jerusalem and Babylonian Talmuds.

JOSHUA BEN LEVI (first half of third century C.E.) Palestinian Amora, mentioned several times as having received the revelation of the Prophet Elijah.

RABBA BAR R. HUNA (d. 322 C.E.) Served as head of the Yeshiva at Sura.

RABBA (BAR NAHAMANI) (c. 270–330) Babylonian Amora, served as head of the Yeshiva at Pumbedita.

RAV (third century C.E.) Babylonian Amora, founder of the Yeshiva at Sura.

RAVA (d. 352 C.E.) One of the most oft-quoted Babylonian Amoraim in the Talmud, led Yeshiva in Mahoza.

RESH (R. SIMEON BEN) LAKISH (third century C.E.) Palestinian Amora, a disciple-colleague of R. Johanan at the Yeshiva in Tiberias.

SAMUEL (MAR) (end of second century to mid-third century) Babylonian Amora, headed the Yeshiva at Nehardea.

ULLA (second half of third century) Palestinian Amora, makes mention in the Talmud of 30 Noahide Commandments.

Sages of the Geonic Period
The Geonim
Sixth to Eleventh Centuries C.E.

AHAI GAON (680–752) Author of She'iltot, originally lived in Babylonia, then moved to Palestine.

NISSIM GAON (c. 990–1062) North African rabbi and leader.

SAADIAH GAON (882–942) Babylonian scholar and author, headed the Yeshiva at Pumbedita.

SAMUEL BEN HOPHNI GAON (d. 1013) Gaon of the Yeshiva at Sura.

Sages of the Middle Ages
The Rishonim
Eleventh to Sixteenth Centuries C.E.

ABRAHAM BEN DAVID OF POSQUIERES (Rabad) (c. 1125–1198) French rabbi, his criticisms on Maimonides' Mishneh Torah appear alongside the latter's text.

ABULAFIA, MEIR (1170?–1244) Spanish rabbi and Talmudic commentator.

BERTINORO, OBADIAH (c. 1450–before 1516) Italian rabbi and Mishnah commentator.

CARO, JOSEPH (1488–1575) Author of the Shulhan Arukh, the authoritative code of Jewish Law in Orthodox Judaism. Also wrote a commentary entitled Kesef Mishneh to Maimonides' Mishneh Torah. Lived in Safed.

ISSERLES, MOSES (1525 or 1530–1572) Known as Rema. Polish rabbi, wrote glosses to Joseph Caro's Shulhan Arukh, which became accepted by Ashkenazic (European) Jewry.

JUDAH HE-HASID (c. 1150–1217) German rabbi; author of Sefer Hasidim, an important source of Jewish laws and customs.

MAHZOR VITRY A work on Jewish liturgy, written by Simhah ben Samuel of Vitry, France, a disciple of Rashi (d. before 1105).

MAIMONIDES, MOSES (1135–1204) Rabbinic codifier and authority, philosopher and physician. Wrote Yad Ha-Chazaka (Mishneh Torah), the most comprehensive codification of Jewish law, as well as a commentary to the Mishnah. Lived in Egypt.

ME'IRI, MENAHEM (1249–1316) French rabbi, wrote Beit Ha-Behirah, a commentary on the Talmud.

NAHMANIDES (Ramban) (1194–1270) Spanish rabbi, philosopher and physician, biblical and Talmudic commentator.

NISSIM BEN REUBEN GERONDI (RAN) (?1310–?1375) Spanish Talmudic commentator.

RADBAZ (DAVID BEN SOLOMON IBN ABI ZIMRA) (1479–1573) Egyptian Talmudist, wrote commentary on Maimonides' Mishneh Torah.

RASHI (R. SOLOMON BEN ISAAC) (1040–1105) French rabbi, the most important rabbinic commentator on the Bible and Talmud.

TAM, JACOB (c. 1100–1171) French rabbi and Tosafist, grandson of Rashi. Wrote the Tosafists' opinion that Trinitarianism is permitted to Gentiles, while forbidden to Jews.

TOSAFISTS A European rabbinic commentary to the Talmud, mainly in the 12th to 14th centuries. Includes the work of many rabbis, especially from Germany and France. In contemporary editions of the Babylonian Talmud, the Tosafists and Rashi's commentary appear alongside the text.

ZACUTO, ABRAHAM (1452–c. 1515) Rabbinic historian and astronomer. Wrote Sefer Ha-Yuhasin, a genealogical work.

Later Rabbinic Sages
The Aharonim
Sixteenth Century to Present

BABAD, JOSEPH (1800–1874/5) Polish rabbi. Wrote Minhat Hinnukh, consisting of discussions on the Commandments.

BACHARACH, JAIR HAYYIM (1638–1702) German rabbi, published responsa Havvat Yair.

BERLIN, NAPHTALI ZEVI JUDAH (1817–1893) Headed the Yeshiva at Volozhin, Russia. Wrote Ha'amek She'elah, a commentary to the She'iltot of R. Ahai Gaon.

CHAJES, ZEVI HIRSCH (1805–1855) Polish rabbi and writer. A recognized Talmudic authority, he pioneered in developing an Orthodox approach to modern scholarly research.

DAVID BEN SAMUEL HALEVY (1586–1667) Polish rabbi. Wrote Turei Zahav (Taz), a commentary on the four parts of the Shulhan Arukh.

EDELS, SAMUEL ELIEZER (1555–1631) Polish rabbi, known as Maharsha, wrote an important commentary to the Talmud.

ELIJAH, GAON OF VILNA (1720–1797) Lithuanian rabbi. One of the greatest Torah scholars of modern times.

EMDEN, JACOB (1697–1776) German rabbi. One of the great rabbinic authorities of his time and author of many books, he was a leader in combatting the heretical Shabbatean movement. He advanced the thesis that Christianity was established by its founders as a religion for the Gentiles, entirely in accordance with the Halakha.

EYBESCHUETZ, JONATHAN (1690/95–1764) German rabbi, wrote important halakhic and homiletic works.

FALK, JACOB JOSHUA (1680–1756) Served as rabbi in Poland and Germany; author of Pnei Yehoshua, a classic commentary to the Talmud; excommunicated the Shabbateans in 1722.

HEILPRIN, JEHIEL (1660–1746) Lithuanian Talmudist and historian. Author of historical work Seder Ha-Dorot.

HIRSCH, SAMSON RAPHAEL (1808–1888) German rabbi, wrote extensively on Orthodox Judaism's views toward modern culture and society.

HYMAN, AARON (1862–1937) English rabbi, wrote a biographical work on the sages of the Talmud.

ISRAEL BA'AL SHEM TOV (c. 1700–1760) Founder of Hasidism in Eastern Europe.

KARBAN HA-EDAH A leading commentary to the Jerusalem Talmud written by David Fraenkel, German rabbi (1707–1762).

LEVI ISAAC OF BERDICHEV (c. 1740–1810) Polish Chassidic rabbi.

LURIA, DAVID (1798–1855) Lithuanian Talmudist and writer. Wrote introduction and commentary to Pirkei D'Rabbi Eliezer.

LURIA, SOLOMON (?1510–1574) Polish Talmudic commentator, known as Maharshal.

LUZZATTO, MOSHE HAYYIM (1707–1746) Italian mystic and writer; wrote Mesillat Yesharim, a classic ethical work.

MARGOLIOT, MOSES (d. 1781) Lithuanian rabbi, wrote commentaries Pnei Moshe and Mareh Ha-Panim on the Jerusalem Talmud.

MEIR SIMHAH HA-KOHEN OF DVINSK (1843–1926) Russian rabbi, wrote Or Same'ah on Maimonides.

MENAHEM AZARIAH OF FANO (1548–1620) Italian rabbi and mystic.

SALANTER, ISRAEL LIPKIN (1810–1883) Founder of the Musar (ethical) movement in Europe.

SOFER, MOSES (1762–1839) Hungarian rabbi and halakhic authority.

SOLOVEITCHIK, JOSEPH B. (1903–   ) American rabbi, ordaining rabbi at R. Isaac Elchanan Theological Seminary of Yeshiva University.

STRASHUN, SAMUEL (1794–1872) Lithuanian rabbi, noted Talmudic commentator.

TIFERET ISRAEL Famed commentary on the Mishnah by R. Israel Lipschutz (1782–1860), German rabbi.

Modern Scholars
Eighteenth to Twentieth Centuries

BACHER, WILHELM (1850–1913) Hungarian scholar, headed a seminary in Budapest.

DERENBOURG, JOSEPH NAPHTALI (1811–1895) French scholar.

EISENSTEIN, JUDAH DAVID (1854–1956) U.S. encyclopedist and anthologist.

FRANKEL, ZACHARIAS (1801–1875) German scholar and historian, wrote Darkei Ha-Mishnah on the Mishnaic era.

GASTER, THEODOR HERZL (1906–   ) American scholar, translated Dead Sea Scrolls into English.

GEIGER, ABRAHAM (1810–1874) German Reformed rabbi.

GINZBERG, LOUIS (1873–1953) American Talmudic scholar, taught at the Jewish Theological Seminary.

GLATZER, NAHUM (1903–   ) American scholar and writer.

GRAETZ, HEINRICH (1817–1891) German scholar, wrote extensively on Jewish history.

KOHLER, KAUFMANN (1843–1926) American Reformed rabbi, served as president of Hebrew Union College.

LEIMAN, SID Professor of Jewish History and Literature at Brooklyn College.

MENDELSSOHN, MOSES (1729–1786) German scholar, philosopher of the Enlightenment movement.

RABIN, CHAIM (1915–   ) Linguist, has written extensively on the Dead Sea Scrolls.

SCHECHTER, SOLOMON (1847–1915) American scholar, served as president of the Jewish Theological Seminary.

SONCINO EDITOR The Soncino edition of the Babylonian Talmud represents the first translation of the Talmud in English.

WEISS, ISAAC HIRSCH (1815–1905) Moravian scholar and writer.